Brekky Central

Behind The Smiles Of Australian Breakfast Television
Adam Boland

EasyRead Large

Copyright Page from the Original Book

MELBOURNE UNIVERSITY PRESS
An imprint of Melbourne University Publishing Limited
11–15 Argyle Place South, Carlton, Victoria 3053, Australia
mup-info@unimelb.edu.au
www.mup.com.au

First published 2014
Text © Adam Boland, 2014
Design and typography © Melbourne University Publishing Limited, 2014

Lyrics from Missy Higgins' 'The Special Two' on page 68. Courtesy Missy Higgins. Lines from Robert Raftery's poem 'Give Fear the Flick' on page 37. Courtesy Robert Raftery.

Cover design by Design By Committee
Typeset in Bembo 12/16pt by Cannon Typesetting
Printed in Australia by McPherson's Printing Group

National Library of Australia Cataloguing-in-Publication entry

Boland, Adam, author.
Brekky central: behind the smiles on Australian breakfast television/ Adam Boland.

9780522867183 (paperback)
9780522867190 (ebook)

Boland, Adam.
Sunrise (Television program; Seven Network, Australia)
The Morning Show (Television program; Seven Network, Australia)
Television producers and directors—Australia—Biography.
Television programs—Australia

791.45023092

TABLE OF CONTENTS

Adam Boland grew up wanting to work in television. By the tender age of 23 he was working at Channel Seven as executive producer of the pre-Olympics program. Three years later Adam was given control of the morning program, *Sunrise,* and Australian breakfast TV changed forever. *Sunrise* quickly became the country's top-rating breakfast show, turning its hosts, Mel and Kochie, into household names and helping two little-known MPs, Kevin Rudd and Joe Hockey hit the big time in politics.

Adam rewrote many of the rules of morning television with his coverage of the Beaconsfield mining tragedy and the introduction of live studio performances. He helped organise *Reach Out to Asia,* a historic primetime concert on the steps of the Sydney Opera House, which raised $20 million for the victims of the Asian tsunami. In 2006, Adam created *The Morning Show,* with hosts Kylie Gillies and Larry Emdur, which instantly became the number-one program in its highly competitive slot. He joined Channel Ten in 2013 as the Network Director of morning television and resigned due to ill-health at the start of January 2014, less than three months after the programs he created, *Wake Up* and *Studio 10* were launched.

Adam is an ambassador for the Australian Foundation for Mental Health Research and Lifeline Canberra.

ACKNOWLEDGEMENTS

Telling this story would not have been possible without people who have much better memories than mine. I'm particularly thankful to Mark Dransfield who, having worked with me at 4BC, Channel Seven and Channel Ten, was able to fill in many gaps.

I wasn't as convinced as MUP's Louise Adler that it was a story worth telling but she was right in suggesting the process could prove cathartic. I'm very glad she wore me down and infected me with her passion.

I'm also thankful she introduced me to Sally Heath who guided me through the maze of writing my first book. Sally provided structure to my thoughts and gently prodded me for better ones. I was very lucky to have such a patient publisher.

Working with copy editor Sarina Rowell was a genuine treat: a first-time author's ideal companion. And the process would not have been complete without editor Louise Stirling and publicist Monica Svarc.

You'll read about people who played key roles in the success of *Sunrise,* but I'd like to thank four others who made me look better than I was: Paul Richards, Monica Lepore, Penny Heath and Bronwyn Martin.

And finally, I'd like to thank my partner, Kenny Ang. He read each chapter and made changes that no doubt saved me from embarrassment. More importantly, he often saves me from my mind. Kenny, once Australia embraces equality, I look forward to calling you my husband.

LAND OF THE GIANTS

'Where the fuck is Adam Boland?'

It was late April 2003 when David Leckie stormed into Channel Seven's Sydney newsroom demanding to know who I was.

Despite having been fired as CEO of Channel Nine more than a year earlier, Leckie was considered a giant in the industry. And a terrifying one. Kerry Stokes felt he was exactly what Seven needed. A big-talking, big-hitting leader who could invoke as much fear in his rivals as he could in his own team.

'Is everyone in here deaf?'

Leckie had only started at Seven the day before, so this was his first visit to the newsroom. Journalists aren't exactly shrinking violets but those present were lost for words. So, instead, they simply pointed. I was worth sacrificing if it meant the giant spared the village.

'Come with me.'

I followed him down one of the cold corridors of what was then Seven's headquarters at Epping. I'd walked them many times, usually in awe. They were lined with black-and-white photos from the shows produced there—everything from *Pick a Box* to *A Country Practice.* I was in awe this time too. Leckie was a towering figure who walked a little like Lurch from *The Addams Family.* I wasn't sure where we were headed and didn't have the courage to ask.

We arrived at Seven's boardroom, where the chief operating officer, David Aspinall, was waiting. This was a man who never smiled; he walked everywhere with a can of Diet Coke in one hand and a balance sheet in the other. I figured his presence wasn't a good sign. Leckie's reign was beginning and that meant old loyalists would need to go. He surely knew the breakfast show I was producing owed its existence to his predecessor, Maureen Plavsic.

'This place is fucked.' Leckie spoke without making eye contact.

I was sitting opposite David Number Two, as he soon became known, who just kept sipping on his half-strength cola. Leckie, meanwhile, was pacing the room like a drill sergeant.

'Your show's okay, but the place is fucked.'

Perhaps I wasn't being fired but, rather, invited to join the revolution.

'Are you ready to have some fun?'

Sure.

He then stopped abruptly in front of me and slammed his hand on the table. For the first time, he looked me in the eye.

'ARE. YOU. READY. TO. HAVE. SOME. FUN?'

YES!

'Let's have some fucking fun.'

1

LIFE BEFORE SEVEN

My addiction to television began when I was nine years old.

My grandparents lived a stone's throw from Channel Seven's studios in Epping, Sydney. During the festive season, I'd look out their window and see the station's broadcast tower lit up like a massive Christmas tree. It was a beacon of hope. A sign that at Seven things were always happy.

I had no way of knowing whether that was true, but I could dream; the magic of television was my version of Willy Wonka's Chocolate Factory. I would often just stare at the building, my favourite TV shows playing out in my head. I would wonder how *Home and Away'*s Summer Bay and *A Country Practice'*s Wandin Valley were both squeezed inside. My dreams of Seven were a constant in my otherwise chaotic childhood.

Mum grew up in the western suburbs of Sydney, and my poppa worked long hours in his taxi to ensure she and her two brothers got a Catholic education. In the summer of 1974, she was eighteen years old. Most weekends, she'd join her friends as they escaped the west and headed straight for the north, to Manly

Beach. They weren't so much interested in the surf, but in smoking, drinking and flirting.

Along the way, she met an older boy named Garry Donovan, who everyone knew as 'Donno'. He was certainly a man of the era, with his long, long hair and pierced left ear. He had a knack for making people laugh, maybe because of his casual approach to life. 'Hello, princess,' was the first thing he ever said to Mum, as he spotted her at a bar. It sounds sleazy, but apparently made her smile.

One night that same year, they ended up at a drive-in theatre. She doesn't remember what movie was playing because, well ... I think you can guess the rest. Nine months later, I arrived. Poppa pressured Mum and Donno down the aisle, but the marriage lasted a matter of weeks. She saw him as her best friend, not her true love. And he didn't disagree.

Seven years on, Mum was determined to leave our housing commission unit and Sydney's western suburbs. Her mission was to find us a better future, despite not knowing how to get it. We stumbled from place to place; every year a new town and, for me, a new school. Getting rather sick of being the new kid in class, for a while I gave up trying to make friends. I didn't really need them. I had something else.

No matter where we lived, my *television* friends from Seven were always there, the people from my dream factory travelling with me. As Mum did shift work to make ends meet, I'd sit at home with *A Country Practice,* watching Brendan and Molly argue, or laughing as Shirl wrestled with a wombat called Fatso. That show opened my eyes to everything from romance to racism. With Seven offering me a form of salvation, it became my unshakable goal to work there one day.

In my lunch hour at primary school, I'd often retreat to the library. Sure, it was a no-go zone for bullies, but it was also a place I could reach for the stars, using nothing but a pen and paper. From the age of eleven, I'd write to just about anyone on the box. No matter which network they worked for, I needed to know *how* they got there.

Many wrote back. *Sunday* reporter Charles Wooley warned me that 'behind all the apparent glamour, there are lots of strains that people in normal 9 to 5 jobs just don't experience. You might be too young to consider this right now, but I have a wife, kids, cats and dogs that I just do not see enough of'. Yes, I was too young to consider that. I would need to learn it the hard way later in life.

The legendary journalist Peter Harvey responded like he was a penpal: 'I am sorry it has taken so long to write. I have been out of the country with Bill Hayden on his trips to China and Tibet.' *Wow,* I thought. *That's cool.* He signed off with 'I hope you get wherever your talent and ambition can take you.'

When I reached high school, stars weren't the only ones to receive my letters. I started hounding programmers and station managers with concepts for shows. Channel Ten's John Lane wrote back to me in 1989, 'When I open your letters, I'm always keen to know "What is this little guy up to now?"'

I studied journalism at the University of Canberra because I wanted to report on our leaders, just like Peter Harvey. Politicians fascinated me. Most had sharp tongues. I remember wishing I could talk like John Button. The senator had a way of ridiculing those who stood in his way, while still making them smile. As it turned out, though, I spent more time with kangaroos than with pollies or journos. The university was stuck in the middle of nowhere, surrounded by bushland.

I didn't finish my degree. My journalism lecturer, Wendy Bilboe, knew I was restless and encouraged me to apply for a cadetship at a Brisbane radio station, 4BC. It wasn't television, but I thought it was surely a step closer to it. 4BC was in the process of reinvention. The station had ditched its country music format in favour of the ambitious task of replicating its sister station—the hugely successful 2UE in Sydney, which was home to talkback kings like John Laws and Alan Jones. Cloning it would require a massive amount of resources: reporters, writers and producers.

I was the most junior of them and was soon getting a crash course in reporting. I worshipped everyone who worked in the 4BC newsroom. They were masters of their craft. One reporter, John Wall, even went to bed with a police scanner. He couldn't sleep unless it was on. With bulletins every thirty minutes, they didn't have time to coddle me. 'Don't use the same word twice in a sentence!' one producer would scream. 'You need to be faster!' another would yell. Before long, I was on my own, writing and reading the news during the graveyard shift, midnight to dawn.

I was a terrible newsreader. 4BC was also Brisbane's rugby league station, so imagine the horror when I went on air and mispronounced the surname of legendary coach Tommy Raudonikis as *Rod-en-eakas*. I also soon discovered that whooping cough was actually pronounced *hooping* cough. Listeners were only too happy to call in to point out my many mistakes. Too, I sounded like a prepubescent choirboy trying his best to be a baritone. Our star presenter at the time was Donna Meiklejohn, who was a guardian of standards, her voice having been refined during a decade at the ABC.

'Did anyone hear our midnight bulletin on Tuesday? Who *was* that reader?' Donna once asked the newsroom.

'Oh, that was me,' I replied excitedly.

There was a short pause before she declared she was off to get a coffee.

For a while, I was on an earlier shift, during the high-rating Stan Zemanek show, which was being syndicated from Sydney. One night, midway through the nine o'clock news, I suddenly realised that I was meant to be reading for ten minutes, but had only prepared a five-minute bulletin. Mark Dransfield, one of my newsroom colleagues, remembers listening to it from home: 'There was dead air for about twenty seconds. Then, all of a sudden, you read another story, before more dead air. You started sounding completely out of breath.'

That's because I was. Between each story, I'd run out of the studio to grab more copy before running back in to read it. It was farcical.

My boss hoped I'd do a better job of reporting than of reading, and assigned me to cover the local council. Brisbane's then Lord Mayor Jim Soorley despised me, thinking I had an agenda against him. I didn't. I was aggressive towards anyone I interviewed. I enjoyed trying to trick people into saying something unexpected and figured that was part of my job. Mayor Jim, though, actually kicked me out of a press conference when I challenged him over new restrictions on business signage. He complained I was out of line for suggesting he was creating signage police. Many years later, he told Fairfax writer Jane Cadzow that I 'was annoying by nature. Always trying to get in the first question, always trying to grandstand and always negative'. He was right on all three counts.

The station manager made it clear to me that I didn't have a future at 4BC. I remember thinking she lacked backbone for refusing to stand up to the mayor, and started looking elsewhere. Television was still out of reach, so I headed to 3AW in Melbourne, where program director and acting news director Steve Price offered me a job as a junior journalist in 1995. He boasted that it was Australia's number one radio station, where strong opinions were valued.

I had only been working in Melbourne for three months when a story flashed on our wire service that Channels Nine and Seven were forming a partnership with Britain's Sky Broadcasting to set up an all-news TV station in Australia. It didn't take long for the boss of Sky News in London, Ian Cook, to find a letter from me on his desk. He forwarded it to Tony Ritchie, who had the job of setting up the Australian service. Tony called to suggest that the next time I was in Sydney, I drop by for a chat. Two days later, I phoned in sick at 3AW and used what little money I had (radio stations don't pay junior journalists well) to buy a plane ticket to Sydney. When I met Tony, my eagerness must have convinced him to hire me, even though Sky News didn't yet have a home.

Over the next few months, I would watch as he turned a suburban warehouse into a futuristic digital newsroom—the likes of which had never been seen in Australia. I was twenty-one years old and had entered television as one of Sky's founding producers. We may have been pioneers, but that meant very few people had heard of us. We would call newsmakers, seeking interviews, only to be greeted with bemusement: 'Why would the horse-racing channel want an interview with me?'

Sky News was also where I had my first brush with media baron Kerry Stokes, as I worked closely with Christine Parker, who was not only one of Sky's first newsreaders but was about to become Stokes's fourth wife. I would often complain to her about things I'd seen on *Seven News.* Sure, I'd never worked in network television but, apparently, I was an expert. She always indulged me, and suggested I write to Stokes, who was Seven's primary shareholder. I'm embarrassed now to read that letter; oh, the arrogance of youth. I told him that some of Seven's bulletins were drowning but he should 'consider me a lifesaver'. I then provided my rather naive manifesto for overhauling his operation, before telling him to 'take me seriously'. Strangely, he did. The phone rang early on a Tuesday morning.

'Who the fuck do you think you are?'

It was Seven's managing director, Gary Rice.

'How would you like it if I posted your letter up on the notice-board in our newsroom?'

His tirade lasted several minutes, and his final words left me heartbroken: 'I run this network and I don't like it when people go behind my back. And, let me tell you, you will never work here.'

Thankfully, he would be proven wrong but my letter wasn't done with me yet. It would come back to bite me almost twenty years later. For now, though, I had to get on with life.

**

Back then, Sky News was staffed only by producers and a reporting job came up at Channel Ten in Cairns. Even though Tony Ritchie thought I was mad to be 'heading to Hickville', it was a place I'd spent time in as a teenager and I was keen to return. Besides, I figured television reporting would be another string to my bow. After telling Ten that I was actually twenty-six years old instead of twenty-three, I became the bureau chief.

Cairns is a complex town. Sugar cane farmers rub shoulders with Chinese tourists, while hippies clash with millionaires over who really owns the rainforest. It's also often the end of the line for people running away from their problems. A mix of the optimistic and the desperate, Cairns is a journalist's dream. For a relatively distant outpost, the bureau was well resourced, with three reporters and three cameramen.

Our beat extended as far north as Papua New Guinea. One Saturday afternoon in mid-1998, the newsroom team was out eating pizza when word came through of an earthquake. That wasn't unusual for PNG, but by the time we ordered our last drinks, we knew this wasn't just any tremor. The ABC reporter in Port Moresby, Sean Dorney, was hearing reports of a tsunami. Aid workers in the country's remote far north were begging for help and feared many people were dead.

Cameraman David Thompson and I decided to head up there, but reaching the area would be tricky, especially on a weekend. Commercial flights would be hit and miss, and wouldn't give us the freedom to roam. A large strip of coast had apparently been hit, so our actual destination was still unclear. We found a Cairns pilot who was willing to take us even though we couldn't answer any of his questions. How long would we be there? Is there a functional airstrip? What about aftershocks? Is it safe to land? We left Cairns first thing on Sunday morning, hoping to find the answers in Port Moresby. It wasn't that simple.

Even though Australians can usually enter PNG without a visa, journalists on a privately chartered plane tend to create suspicion. Immigration officials wanted paperwork. They couldn't tell us what kind but it was something more than we had—which was nothing. I tried to distract them with a call to arms: 'We must get to Vanimo. Australia has sent us to cover the tsunami.' They again asked for the paperwork.

I looked to David for advice. He'd worked in these parts for years, so I hoped he'd know what to do. He smiled and settled in for a nap. 'We're on PNG time now,' was his astute observation. The reports from the country's northern tip were becoming increasingly descriptive and increasingly bad, but there seemed no sense of emergency here in the capital. *More reason,* I thought, *to get moving.* It was clear people needed pictures to understand.

We finally departed just after lunch for what would be the scariest flight of my life. About an hour after taking off, the plane's windows frosted up and the cabin started to vibrate. David and I looked out the window to see trees just metres below. Our plane was struggling to clear PNG's rugged hinterland. I closed my eyes and gripped my seat. *Should we just jump out? We'll never be found. Oh God, I love my family.* It took a good ten minutes for the rattling to stop and for the pilot to yell out, 'It's all good!' His reassurance only confirmed that we'd had a close call.

We arrived in the Vanimo disaster zone late on Sunday afternoon, to be greeted by chaos. The grass runway was surrounded by locals, waiting for word from friends and family in outlying villages. The injured were being piggybacked to a makeshift triage. I managed to grab the attention of a nurse, who told me that thousands of people were unaccounted for. *Thousands.* Rather than feeling helpless, I felt an instant need to report. An instant need to tell people what we were seeing. It's times like these that the role of a journalist becomes vital. They sound the call for help. As David started shooting, I tried to contact Ten's newsroom in Sydney. When I finally got through, a junior staffer suggested I call back after the nightly news. I sighed and got back to work. I have no memory of where we slept that night. Given the events, I guess it doesn't matter. I do remember that the locals went out of their way to make us feel welcome even during their time of crisis.

By morning, Australians were waking to news of a major emergency. The few reporters on the ground were able to relay stories by phone, but getting pictures out wasn't as easy. There were no satellite dishes or feed points in that part of the world. We had to do it the slow way—get back on the plane for the almost three-hour trip back to Port Moresby, where the ABC allowed us to use its bureau. On that first return shuttle, we flew low over a lagoon clogged by bodies. Pigs would later feast on the remains. Here was one moment when I did feel helpless. I closed my eyes in an effort to disconnect from the scene. When we walked through Port Moresby Airport, it was obvious where we'd been. We were covered in dirt, our faces were drained and we were towing our camera gear. Then we walked past someone I'd idolised for years.

To cover the disaster, Seven had sent seasoned reporter Chris Reason, who was in the terminal working the phones, trying to find a way to get up to Vanimo. There were no commercial flights and charters were near impossible to get. He saw us and slammed down the phone.

'Where have you guys come from?'

'Vanimo.'

'How did you get there?'

'We have a plane out the front.'

'Fuck. Can I hitch a ride?'

'Sure, if you pick up the bill.'

Even back then, Ten didn't spend much on news. As bureau chief, I was conscious of budgets, and was conscious that here was an opportunity to cover the story at Seven's expense. Seven had very deep pockets, as did its bitter rival, Nine.

Vanimo was soon home to dozens of reporters, producers and cameramen. Channel Nine even sent a private plane, with its very own satellite equipment, from Sydney. David and I eagerly awaited reinforcements from Ten, which arrived in the form of a lone political reporter from Brisbane.

The Vanimo Hospital was a basic building, not far from the airstrip. It normally catered for fifty patients but was now overflowing, with hundreds. Despite the tropical heat, there was no air-conditioning—ceiling fans just pushed hot air from one side of the room to the next. Patients who couldn't fit inside the hospital were left lying under tarpaulins on the lawn. Many had lost limbs, and others would as gangrene took hold. We watched as one man brought in his injured child. He'd buried his wife just hours earlier.

The person at the centre of this mess was Dr John Novette. He'd been playing snooker when the wave struck, and from that moment on, he'd been working. Three days straight now, with little sleep. That didn't worry him; his biggest concern was running out of blood and bandages. I watched as he went from bed to bed. No matter what he found, he remained calm and even smiled when he could. I asked how he coped. He quietly responded that he had no choice.

With such humble heroes there, providing hope, it was hard to stomach the suggestion that a media crew was getting in the way. Rumours spread through the camp that a reporter and cameraman had boarded the last chopper out of a forward treatment station for victims, possibly taking places meant for the injured. *The Courier Mail'* s Brendan O'Malley tried to confirm the story by speaking to those present, including doctors, a local governor and a Catholic priest. None of them could be certain the claims were true, so O'Malley decided not to report them. The reporter, in the meantime, had heard from his bosses that O'Malley had been asking questions. He confronted him at the camp and threatened to slap him with a defamation suit. The exchange became increasingly heated, and when I came to O'Malley's defence, the television reporter told me to fuck off back to school.

My experience in Vanimo was, indeed, a lesson, especially in the power of the media. More than 2500 people lost their lives in the tsunami but that toll would have been higher had reporters not communicated the need for aid. Although the tsunami was clearly a story that mattered, there was no reason reporting on it would get me national attention. But, later that year, I had a most unexpected encounter—the result of some useful contacts and a rather bad wardrobe—that did.

***

In 1998 Jerry Seinfeld jetted off to Australia, having just recorded the very last episode of his iconic sitcom. The country's showbiz reporters were on his tail every step of the way, but had to make do with occasional shots of him being whisked away in a black van. No interviews. In fact, hardly a wave.

The final leg of Seinfeld's Australian holiday brought him to Far North Queensland, as he'd booked the penthouse at the Mirage resort in Port Douglas. I spent a few days chasing him around for Channel Ten, mainly speaking with people who claimed to have spotted him. It was the story you have when you don't have a story. Just as we were about to give up, cameraman Rick Sproxton received a call from a pilot mate at the airport, who'd heard that Seinfeld was about to fly out.

We were the only TV crew there when he walked on to the runway. Finally, a wave! We knew we'd struck gold. But, just as we'd packed up our tripod, a man came running at us from the plane. *Shit, had we done something wrong?* It was Seinfeld's manager, calling me to the fence.

'Hey, kid. Jerry wants to speak to you.'

'What? Yeah, sure. Can I bring my cameraman?'

'Yes, hurry up.'

It was all rather surreal. I shook Seinfeld's hand and then asked him the first thing that came to mind.

'Why me?'

'It was your tie. I felt sorry for you. I thought, *This kid's put on a tie. And it's a knit-tie. Completely out of fashion.* I thought, *This kid needs a break.'*

My follow-up question was as inspired as my first.

'So, what do I ask the world's funniest man?'

'Now I have to do your job for you? Giving you a break is not enough?'

Those first two answers were soon beamed around the world. I became known as the kid with the bad tie. At first, I enjoyed the attention. There was radio interview after radio interview. While waiting to chat live to Andrew Denton, I told him I was surprised by the response. He confided in me: 'Ah yes, but, Adam, Australia is an easy fuck.'

It's fair to say I had a very thin skin, though. Being the subject of press or commentary was foreign to me, and I took anything that was said about me extremely personally. TV shows on all networks had shown the clip, with many people mocking me for my questions. *The Today Show'*s Tracy Grimshaw scoffed to co-host Steve Liebmann that I'd squandered a big opportunity. *That's it,* I thought. *I've had enough.* I fired off a defensive note, telling her there was more to the interview than a bad tie and some silly questions. (Actually, I'm not sure there was.) In what was either an act of attempted mentorship or just arose out of a desire to slap me, Grimshaw tracked me down to deliver a clear message: get a grip. 'We all have those moments. I've had those moments. Imagine walking into a hotel hallway naked after confusing it for the bathroom.' She'd apparently had a rather big night at the 1998 Logie Awards. In a way, her shame helped ease mine.

***

I had a genuinely good time in Cairns. I loved the team and I loved the journalistic extremes that were part of the job. I would have stayed longer had it not been for a spectacular meltdown—the first of many that would come to punctuate my career.

It was 1999 and I'd just turned twenty-four. I was drinking with other members of the Cairns media at a monthly get-together. It was getting late and I'd been up early, reading the news on a breakfast radio show before doing a full day at Ten. I was tired, but that's no excuse for what happened next.

I became agitated about one of my cameramen having a drink with a colleague from the opposition. And, yes, I was conveniently ignoring the fact that mixing with our rivals was the entire point of the night. I accused him of betrayal—both personal and professional—before storming out in dramatic style.

That would have been fine had I not come across a car belonging to our rival. I'm not an overly physical or coordinated person, but I somehow found the strength to fly through the air with what witnesses called a karate kick (I think they gave me too much credit). That kick caused damage. So much so, that police were called.

I wasn't there to greet them. By that stage, I'd stumbled a few blocks, apparently screaming at anyone in my eyeline. My only memory of that night is of walking in front of oncoming traffic along the Cairns Esplanade. Cars swerved to miss me, while startled backpackers helped me to safety. I don't know whether it was an unconscious suicide attempt or just a drunken lapse. I was certainly off my face. Generously, the Channel Ten cameraman who triggered my outburst tracked me down and got me safely home. By the next morning, the police had caught up with me. I was arrested and charged with wilful damage.

Looking back at that episode, it's clear to me and my doctors that I was showing the first signs of bipolar disorder. Mum had noticed my mood swings when I was a teenager, but now my behaviour was more erratic. The charges were later dismissed, but it didn't matter. Ten, quite rightly, argued that I had brought the company into disrepute.

My northern adventure was over.

2

THE DREAM FACTORY

Everyone needs a guardian angel. Mine was Tony Ritchie. When Channel Ten showed me the door, my former Sky News boss opened a new one. And it was the one I'd dreamed of walking through since childhood.

In 2000, Tony was deputy news director at Channel Seven in Sydney. Having somehow heard about my tropical meltdown, he threw me a lifeline. Seven needed a producer to take care of its in-flight news bulletins for Ansett. Not only did Tony offer me the job, he hired my best friend from Cairns, Steven Claus, as an editor. We arrived for our first day of work on Monday, 21 February 2000.

Seven's Epping headquarters was a television city. Even the entrance was reminiscent of the big Hollywood studios; you'd need to state your business before guards opened the boom gate. Once inside, it was wise to stay off the roads. There were lighting trucks, news cars, and a semi-trailer packed full of the equipment needed to televise major events like the Australian Open. The Seven fleet was so big that the station had its own petrol bowsers. I couldn't have been happier. I wasn't just a kid in any old candy store. I'd finally made it inside Willy Wonka's factory.

As we walked towards the building, the Channel Seven helicopter took off from beyond the tennis court. Yes, a tennis court. Legend has it that beneath the court lay hundreds of tapes from early Seven productions like *The Mavis Bramston Show.* The station apparently ran out of room in its library, so used the tapes as landfill. If true, it shows a blatant disregard for television history.

Steven and I waited in reception, surrounded by photos of the network's stars. We killed time by trying to name as many as we could. It became clear the term 'star' was used pretty loosely. Tony Ritchie soon appeared, with his trademark grin resembling that of a naughty schoolboy who'd just gotten away with a prank. He reminded me that I was the one who'd been naughty: 'Whatever you do, don't kick any of our cars.'

He led us down corridors, up and down stairs and then, finally, through the kind of doors you'd find in a run-down hospital ward. The building was a maze—the result of multiple extensions over the years, as more and more shows moved in. I felt intimidated when I walked into the newsroom. It couldn't have been more different from my old workplace in Cairns, which had only just got access to the internet. The main production line consisted of fifteen producers who faced each other. At the end of their long, arched desk was a wall of nine television screens tuned not just to their rivals but to overseas news channels like CNN. When not on the road, reporters had their own desks to the right of the producers. Some used their relative privacy to call sources and hunt down leads. Others used it to check their hair and re-apply makeup.

At the opposite end of the room was a platform used by people with a tendency to shout. They were the chiefs-of-staff, responsible for directing reporters and camera crews to the scene of breaking stories. Given the unpredictable nature of news, it wasn't the easiest of jobs. They weren't just shouting because of the stress they were under but to be heard over the incessant police and ambulance scanners. Filming these guys in action would have made good reality television.

Out the back, you'd find the engine room, known as news exchange, where vision would come in from around the country and around the world. The operators there were just as stressed as the chiefs-of-staff. As one feed of pictures ended, another would start. They'd often need to record eight things at once, while logging all of them in a computer. It was noisy and chaotic, and not a place for the faint-hearted.

Pretty much everyone in the newsroom was working on just three bulletins a day: the morning news, the six o'clock news and the late night news. The flagship was 6pm, which had priority. The other two had to wait their turn for resources. Imagine, then, how the Ansett news service was treated. It wasn't even in the queue. My new role would resemble a seagull darting in and out for whatever scraps were left. I didn't care. I was working at Channel Seven. I was lining up for coffee alongside stars from *Home and Away,* walking past the set of *Wheel of Fortune* and rubbing shoulders with the likes of Chris Reason (though I suspect he didn't notice). As far as I was concerned, I'd made it.

Producing Ansett news was simple: you'd just pinch whatever stories you liked from Seven's other bulletins. You could even copy and paste scripts and nobody would notice. A newsreader would then sit in front of a camera for a few minutes to read the introductions, without ever seeing the actual stories. We never went near a studio or a control room. The whole thing was put together in an edit suite. That made it cheap. The production team consisted of just two people: an editor and a producer. In the case of the late shift, that was Steven Claus and myself.

I tried to keep out of the way of the other newsroom producers. I spent most of my time at a desk near the news exchange, watching material come in from overseas. Of the hours of pictures being fed, little more than a minute of them would ever make it to air. Commercial television was always more interested in a suburban McDonald's being robbed than in a refugee crisis in the Middle East.

But that gave me an idea.

I started including any stories that interested me, in the hope that it interested others. Catering to yourself is not considered the best method of producing television, but what did I care? Rather than sitting through regurgitated day-old local news, passengers on Ansett were suddenly given the world. I felt like a journalist again, instead of a secretary.

Something else happened that would have a profound impact on my career: I realised I liked hearing other people say my words, especially people who had a gift for presenting. There are some presenters who sit in front of a camera and just read whatever is on the autocue. There are others who don't just read but interpret the words. They make the viewer *feel* what they're saying. I was lucky to work with two such people—Chris Bath and Georgie Gardner.

They had different styles, so I started writing to suit each of them. That meant sharp and punchy copy for Chris, and measured, more expressive words for Georgie. I think it was then that I finally understood what it meant to be a producer. Working with people like them amplifies your storytelling; they made viewers pay attention. From that point on, I no longer cared about being on camera or behind a microphone. I was proud to call myself a producer.

It was thanks to Chris and Georgie that I started to get noticed. Both talked me up to Seven's then director of news, Ian Cook—the same Ian Cook who referred me to Tony Ritchie at Sky News back in 1995. Cookie was known by some to be a smiling assassin, and it's true he could instil fear but usually in those who deserved it. I only ever found him to be honest and nurturing. But I was still scared shitless every time he called me to his office.

In mid-April 2000, he asked whether I'd be interested in producing a new incarnation of the early morning bulletin, *Sunrise.* It had been around in one form or another since the early 1990s. It was rarely given much love and was never seen as a competitor to Channel Nine's *Today,* which had dominated the slot for two decades with well-respected journalists interviewing celebrities and newsmakers. Come 2000, *Sunrise* was little more than a ninety-minute news bulletin wedged between cartoons and a music video show. It was there simply to enhance perceptions that Channel Seven offered the same amount of news as Nine.

Cookie was straight up: there'd be no increase in pay, the hours would be shocking and it was unlikely we'd have a hell of a lot more viewers than caught an Ansett flight each day.

'I'll take it!'

For me, it was a chance to work in a control room with live news and on a major network, as opposed to on a plane. I'd even have a small team of assistant producers. There was an added benefit: the show would be co-hosted by one of my favourite presenters,

Georgie Gardner. The male host would be someone I'd never met: Mark Beretta, a sports reporter from Melbourne. That worried me. What would a sports reporter know about news? And I knew nothing about sport. Would we have anything in common? The first time we met, it was clear he had concerns too. I could tell by his face that he was unsettled by my age. To be fair, I did look twelve.

The first edition of *Seven News Sunrise* went to air on 1 May 2000. Just as with the Ansett news, I wanted to push the envelope. I was rostered on to start at midnight but would always be in the newsroom by 7pm. Dinner each night consisted of a Big Mac and a Coke (I developed kidney stones three times during my early years at Seven). I'd eat while getting across the news from every state, as well as scanning my beloved overseas feeds. I was always keen to lead with something different from either the *Late News* or the 6pm bulletins. Viewers needed to feel they were being told something new, even if few things had actually happened overnight. In truth, though, plenty happened overnight in other parts of the world and the time differences made it perfect fodder. My producers spent most of their time lining up live crosses with reporters from CNN and NBC. Georgie and Mark ended up speaking to some of the biggest names in television news, coming to them from places like Tel Aviv, Washington and Moscow. They loved it and so did I. The three of us became very close.

Ian Cook must have been impressed. Three months in, he cherry-picked me to play a major role in the televising of the Sydney Olympic Games. The Olympics were a big deal not just for Sydney but for Seven; the network was host broadcaster and needed to get it right. Coverage would begin well before the opening ceremony, with an ambitious plan to follow the Olympic flame. For two weeks, we'd provide live coverage as the torch was handed from runner to runner, in small country towns, up and down mountains and, finally, taken into the heart of Sydney. I was asked to take charge of a daily afternoon show called *Follow the Flame* while *Sunrise* was sidelined for other Olympic programming.

It got better. The first week of shows would be hosted by Chris Bath, and the second by Georgie and Mark. I was also allowed to recruit Steven Claus to work on the production. If I was going to be out of my comfort zone, I wanted people I knew to come along for the ride. *Follow the Flame* would also be the first time I worked with senior producer Matt Clarke and reporter Monique Wright. Both would later play major roles in the success of *Sunrise.*

Channel Seven was renowned for its technical innovations. It was Seven that first placed cameras inside cars as they raced around Mount Panorama in Bathurst. That was in 1979. RaceCam, as it was known, was soon adopted for motor sports around the world. More than twenty years later, we used similar thinking in following the flame. We drove a

Winnebago just in front of whoever was running with the torch. Its back door was kept open, so our cameraman could shoot every second of the action. From there, the pictures were beamed to the Channel Seven helicopter that was always flying above. The chopper then relayed the vision back to the studio.

'It was a technical feat, but things still went wrong,' says Matt Clarke. 'We actually lost the signal, ironically, as the flame was carried up the street alongside Channel Seven. We'd followed the thing from Canberra to Sydney but lost sight of it over our own back fence.'

A few thousand people carried the torch around New South Wales, which meant the editorial challenge was almost as big as the technical one. There was no way of knowing who'd have hold of the torch at any given time. We had to prepare biographical backgrounds on almost all of them, just in case we took a shot of them during our live coverage. There would have been nothing worse than Chris, Georgie or Mark being lost for words while commentating.

We identified each runner by the number on his or her shirt. So, 1106 could be a famous athlete or 2408 might be a well-known politician. Chances are, though, it would merely be one of the hundreds of people who got to run because they worked for an Olympic sponsor like AMP. It was pretty hard to make a mid-level manager from a bank sound interesting. But, each day, there were also torchbearers guaranteed to inspire, and there was no better example than Eliza Stankovic.

A week after her sixteenth birthday, meningococcal disease cost Eliza her legs and the fingers on both hands. She spent more than a fortnight in a coma and six months in hospital. Her parents never left her side. Three years on, she was determined to make them proud by carrying the torch through Bowral. The running didn't worry her. Her prosthetic legs were serving her well. The challenge, she thought, was making sure she didn't drop it.

Reporter Paul Marshall described her run during a live cross to Chris Bath. 'She held that torch so tightly,' he said before suddenly stopping mid-sentence. He tried again. 'So tightly,' but he again had to look away. Paul, a veteran of news reporting, was trying not to cry. Such was the power of the Olympic flame. This wasn't a meaningless relay. It had a genuine spirit that united people through its message of hope and resilience.

Paul met many of the runners. 'I never carried the flame,' he tells me, 'but I ran a bloody long way alongside it.' And not all those who carried the torch ran. The first to hold it one morning when it was near Canberra was a man in a wheelchair. Paul remembers: 'It was still dark and pouring, bucketing rain, but as he pushed out onto the road with the torch in his hand, he just had the biggest smile on his face.' The man was soaked by the end but still smiling. Also smiling were those who lined the relay route, among them a blind man waiting on his porch. 'He told me he wouldn't be able to see it go by,' says Paul, 'but he just wanted to be there when it did.'

Everything was going well; each day's show brought new characters and new stories. But the biggest test would come on Thursday, 15 September 2000. That was not only the day before my twenty-fifth birthday but the eve of the opening ceremony. Our show that night would be a two-hour extravaganza in primetime. And, more than that, it would likely be watched by just about everyone in the country, as the Olympic flame arrived in Sydney. Some of Australia's biggest names would carry it through the city, including Olivia Newton-John, Steve Waugh and Pat Rafter.

Georgie and Mark would be hosting from a harbourside home that looked straight at the Opera House (and that had been leased by Seven for its chief executive, Julian Mounter, before he'd abruptly left the company almost a year earlier). But I wanted added punch. Golfing great Greg Norman was in Australia, to carry the torch over the Harbour Bridge. That was happening earlier in the day, so, in theory, he'd be available to co-host our night-time coverage. I started talking with his people a fortnight before the broadcast. They didn't rule it out but refused to confirm right up until just two days out. In the end, it was my rather melodramatic plea that got it across the line. With the best quavering voice I could feign, I told his minder my job depended on Greg Norman's appearance. It didn't, but she wasn't to know.

'Please, you need to do this for me. *Please.'*

Norman was locked in but with strict conditions. A water taxi had to pick him up from the Park Hyatt hotel in The Rocks. He'd spend no longer than fifteen minutes with us before taking the water taxi back. We were told he had another appointment immediately afterwards. The water taxi driver was worried he'd never find the right house, so Ian Cook's assistant, Paula Crawford, volunteered to wait on the jetty with a massive Channel Seven umbrella. Norman turned up right on cue.

The crowd in central Sydney that night was massive—police put it at close to a million. People were lined twenty-deep. We had reporters, including Paul Marshall and Chris Reason, every 100 metres. Monique Wright would be on board the Winnebago as the flame navigated its way down George Street. I was back in the main control room at Channel Seven, where I could see every camera and speak to every reporter. I'd be telling Mark and Georgie where to cross and when.

About thirty minutes before we went to air, I ran outside and vomited in the car park. I didn't know if I was ready for something this big. I remember thinking, *Don't they know how old I am?* My nerves would need to take a back seat, though. Once the show starts, there's no way out. It's like a rollercoaster. As the opening credits rolled, I was strapped in and ready to scream.

We came on air just as Italian tenor Andrea Bocelli stood proudly with the flame, beneath the sails of the Opera House. 'The Olympic flame has arrived in the Olympic city,' announced Mark Beretta. Olivia Newton-John then ran the torch in a loop around the Opera House before meeting up with Pat Rafter. As their two torches kissed, fireworks exploded over Sydney, and the giant Olympic rings on the Harbour Bridge lit up for the first time. Our cameras captured it all. We went from our chopper to shots of the cheering crowd, and then up close to Pat Rafter as he began his run alongside the harbour. It really was spectacular.

Things got tricky, though, as the torch reached George Street. The noise was deafening. Monique Wright could hardly hear me. I was screaming 'START TALKING!' down her earpiece. She still couldn't make out what I was saying but took a punt. Her live reporting captured the scene beautifully. Just as with Paul Marshall a few days earlier, you could hear the emotion in her voice.

As the flame was passed to cricketer Steve Waugh, a Channel Nine cameraman blocked our shot. He'd somehow wedged between our Winnebago and the torch in a clear breach of the broadcast rules. I was ropable. I got on the open talkback and yelled to every Seven staffer along the route: 'GET THAT FUCKING CUNT OUT OF OUR SHOT!'

I then felt a hand on my shoulder. I didn't realise that Seven's Sydney boss, Geoff Hill, had been standing behind me. I thought I'd overstepped the line, but he just looked at me and said, 'You're doing well, son.'

Back at Lavender Bay, Greg Norman had been with Georgie and Mark for a lot longer than the agreed fifteen minutes. *He* was the one who wanted to stay. 'I can't believe how good this is,' he told our viewers. 'It just makes you so proud to be an Australian.' The water taxi driver wasn't sharing his passion. He had another job to get to and was threatening to leave Norman behind. Paula Crawford was doing all she could to make him stay. 'I physically held onto the boat so it couldn't leave without Greg,' she remembers. 'Stressful much?'

Ian Cook called soon after we came off air. 'Well, that seemed to go well,' he said in his understated way. It had gone so well that I almost vomited again in relief.

As soon as the Olympics were over, it was back to our little early morning bulletin. But, unbeknown to me, moves were afoot for a revolution at dawn.

3

THE SUN RISES

In November 2000, Maureen Plavsic became the first woman to run an Australian television network when she was named chief executive of Channel Seven. The former boss of sales was determined to bring new energy to Seven, unveiling new shows and even a new logo. But, sadly for Plavsic, reality soon set in. Reality television, that is.

Channel Ten's *Big Brother* was the only show anyone was talking about. Younger demographics were glued to it. Plavsic couldn't understand the phenomenon and insisted she didn't know anyone who watched it. Perhaps that was the problem. Seven had lost touch with a significant chunk of the television audience. With primetime proving a challenge, Plavsic started looking at the other end of the day, seeing it as an untapped reserve of revenue. She was sick of us using a toy gun at breakfast. It was time to throw a grenade.

In late 2001, senior creatives (including Tim Worner, who is now Seven's chief executive) devised a plan to take on the firmly entrenched *Today* on Channel Nine. They drew much inspiration from the talk show *Fox & Friends* that was proving a hit for America's

Fox News Channel. No expense would be spared. The multi-million dollar production would outstrip what is spent on breakfast television even today. The show would get a dedicated studio, and be fronted by Andrew Daddo and Lisa Forrest.

Big money. Big hosts. Big deal.

Given my, albeit short, experience with breakfast television, I was invited to be one of almost twenty producers involved. As line producer, my job would be to put the show to air each morning from the control room. That suited me. It was where I had the most fun. Matt Clarke from *Follow the Flame* would be the new show's supervising producer, and we'd all report to executive producer Charlie Wood, who'd come from the lifestyle program *Sydney Weekender.*

In February 2002, and with four weeks before the show's debut, Tim Worner walked into our production office with a carton of beer. The network's board had changed its mind, believing the money could be better spent elsewhere. We'd been axed without even getting on air. We were devastated. We'd put so much work into the format and been keen to show it off. This ordeal served as a valuable lesson that there is no security in television.

Thankfully for Matt and me, we were invited back to the unloved *Sunrise* news bulletin. We joked that nobody else wanted the gig. But I was no longer in charge. Charlie Wood was under contract when his show was axed, so he ended up joining us as well.

While I still called the shots in the control room, he was now the boss. I wasn't happy. As much as I liked Charlie, his background was lifestyle and entertainment, not serious news. Why should I play second fiddle in my own domain? Ian Cook sympathised but insisted his hands were tied.

The changes weren't isolated to behind the scenes. Georgie Gardner and Mark Beretta were both promoted to the 6pm news, but on different networks. Georgie switched to Channel Nine to present the weather, while Mark was tapped to read the sport on Seven. Amid all the upheaval, there was, I felt, one upside: I'd be working with Chris Reason. He was named the new host of *Sunrise* alongside former *Today Tonight* presenter Melissa Doyle. Reaso had impressed Kerry Stokes while steering Seven's breaking news coverage of the 9/11 attacks on America the previous year.

But, from day one, the new *Sunrise* dynamic was broken, both on and off the air.

I disagreed with just about anything Charlie proposed. I felt he never understood the complexity of the rundown, suggesting lifestyle stories for our seven o'clock news hour that were better suited to after 8am, when the show's format became more casual. To me, the show was struggling to balance light and shade.

Reaso, too, was having difficulties, but mainly with himself. He found it challenging to segue from the serious to the trivial. One moment he'd be required to talk about tension in the Middle East and the next about the best way to make coffee. Breakfast television may look like an easy genre but most find it difficult to master.

Reaso envied Mel's level of ease on air but had a bigger and potentially crippling reservation: he didn't respect her as a journalist (at least, not then). He'd spent twenty-five years reporting from the frontline of wars and natural disasters. Sitting alongside Mel just didn't feel right to him. And it showed on air. It also took me time to build a rapport with Mel. She didn't know me all that well and could sense my adulation for Reaso. We all staggered forward in the hope something would click into gear.

And, with time, the show did start to find its feet. We handled breaking news particularly well: Reaso didn't need to smile or feign interest in cooking, so was firmly in his comfort zone, and Mel injected a powerful human dimension. People in television news tend to become desensitised but she was genuinely moved by human tragedy. Reaso started to appreciate her method of storytelling (and now considers her to be one of Australia's great broadcasters).

But, despite some internal momentum, nobody was paying much attention. With its regimented format, the show would never be a serious competitor for *Today.* As far as the network was concerned, the slot was surrendered as soon as plans for Charlie's big show were scrapped. It was no surprise then that

Charlie decided to leave in late 2002. He'd merely been serving out his contract and, by his own admission, was glad to be getting on with his life. I was again placed in charge.

It *was* a surprise, though, when Chris Reason had to leave.

On the night of Wednesday, 9 October 2002, doctors revealed they'd found a tumour behind Reaso's kidney. He shared the news with me straight after the show on Thursday. I didn't know what to say. In fact, I apparently said almost nothing at all. He later told me my silence both angered and hurt him. Most of his mates had given him words of assurance and urged him to be strong. He felt my reaction meant I knew something more about the cancer than he did: that things were a lot worse than he thought.

In truth, I think I was just in shock. I looked up to few people the way I did to Chris Reason and couldn't stand the thought of him falling. I tried to phone him later but had to hang up mid-call after again failing to find the right words. I understand how he perceived my reaction as a lack of empathy. Perhaps, to some extent, it was a sign of my emotional immaturity.

Reaso vowed he would return. But, in the meantime, we had to find someone to fill his chair. As Channel Seven's finance editor, David Koch had been a regular contributor to *Sunrise.* He'd even hosted the bulletin for a while, back in 1996. He was never your usual finance reporter. He was once chided for asking a reporter on air whether she had got a lei while covering a meeting of world leaders in Hawaii. She stumbled through her answer while refusing to acknowledge his sexual innuendo. Given his close association with *Sunrise,* he was the obvious choice to cover for Reaso during his treatment.

The show instantly had a different dynamic. Kochie never took himself as seriously as Reaso. He didn't spend an hour researching before interviews. In fact, I'd often brief him while he walked to the studio. He was cheery on air and clicked well with Mel, but the format didn't allow him much space to be himself. He was like a jack-in-the-box that hadn't yet been cranked.

In mid-November, I put together a proposal that would completely change the format. I never liked the idea of *Sunrise* being dismissed as an afterthought and felt we had the right talent in front of, and behind, the camera to start pushing boundaries. Even if it didn't work, Matt Clarke and I figured, we'd have fun trying.

Every good breakfast show has some key ingredients. The first is a news update every thirty minutes. And it can never be late. Timepoor viewers use them as signposts. They expect to see the headlines at 7am, for example, knowing they'll still have time to catch the seven-fifteen bus to work. The second is big interviews—be they with newsmakers or entertainers. Celebrities tend to get pushed to later in the show, in the hope viewers will stick around to watch. The average person tunes in for less than fifteen minutes, so, for ratings-hungry producers, every extra minute counts. And the third is a less formal presenting style than that of, say, the 6pm news. Most people want to start the day with a smile and will simply switch off if things get too serious (with the exception of days when big news is breaking).

Our new plan would still factor in all three ingredients but also include what were, back then, some dramatic points of difference. Kochie and Mel would rely less on scripts and more on talking points. They'd debate the issues of the day, rather than just report them. And, crucially, our audience would heavily influence the choice of issues. Journos thinking something was important didn't automatically mean people agreed. Instead of just lecturing our viewers, we were keen to hear what they thought. It was a lesson from my days at talkback radio stations, and an approach that had not been adopted in television. Social media was yet to give viewers a voice.

Ian Cook had seen me experiment before by changing the production style of Ansett news, and was happy to let us play, but only if we first got sign-off from Maureen Plavsic. The chief executive still had an active interest in the slot after failing to get it overhauled almost a year earlier. She was instantly taken by the proposal but worried about what her programmers would think. Cookie reminded her that the news division was its own entity and the programmers didn't need to be involved. They never thought all that much of news, and he feared they could veto our plan. Our case was pretty straightforward: 'What do you have to lose?' We weren't asking for more money or otherwise proposing anything as extravagant as Charlie's never-to-be-seen show. All we needed was her approval for our presenters to be themselves; something still considered bold, and even reckless, for news-based shows at the end of 2002. She gave us six months for it to work.

I took Kochie and Mel to lunch at Lindfield on Sydney's upper north shore to walk them through the format. I had endless sheets of paper describing every second of the rundown; the kind of minute detail that only a producer would find interesting. Mel questioned something called 'the soapbox' that kept appearing on every page. I wanted to use that segment to read out emails from viewers and for Kochie and Mel to share their own views on the news of the day. Mel looked at me in near horror: 'Why would anyone care what we think?' She'd been trained to be impartial, and valued her reputation as a journalist and newsreader. Kochie, on the other hand, embraced this approach. He'd once hosted a breakfast radio show, so was more than comfortable with being himself and interacting with the audience. Had Mel not been Kochie's long-time friend, I suspect she would've opted out.

Maureen Plavsic was on board, Ian Cook was on board and the hosts were on board. The same couldn't be said for the rest of the network. We not only felt like outsiders, we really were. We weren't regarded as important enough to be given office space inside the main building, so were relegated to a two-storey demountable alongside the car park. The tin shed, as it became known, wasn't the most luxurious place to work. During summer, it got stinking hot; and during winter, it was nearly impossible to get warm. Wet weather was the worst. There wasn't any cover between the main building and ours, so we inevitably got wet. Steven Claus, who'd been assigned to the unit as our senior editor, once fell down the shed's steps, which became a slippery dip when it rained.

There were some in the newsroom who would've been happy for the entire show to disappear. 'They saw us as more of a nuisance than anything useful,' remembers Matt Clarke. 'They certainly didn't help us with resources or facilities, and weren't really sharing a lot of information.'

We didn't care. We knew our target audience and it wasn't the newsroom. We wanted viewers who'd deserted morning television for radio. Although it was perceived as an institution, we felt the *Today* show had turned many people off the slot.

We weren't the only ones who thought so. Peter Meakin was Nine's head of news and current affairs at the time, and ultimately responsible for *Today.* He tells me: 'The show was moribund. It took itself miles too seriously. It had one host in particular who took himself incredibly seriously. It was summed up one day by an interview they had with Robin Williams. The comedian was his riotous self. It was absolutely out of control. I was rolling on the floor laughing. It was great, hilarious television and the compere said, "If we can be serious for a moment." It brought it all to a grinding halt. That pretty much summed up the show.'

That compere was respected journalist Steve Liebmann, who, along with Tracy Grimshaw, guided viewers through what their producers considered the main stories of the day. As Gerald Stone wrote in his book *Who Killed Channel Nine?,* the show 'seemed to be growing more and more insulated from the topics viewers really cared about, although up until then it had been largely protected from any backlash by the lack of serious opposition'.

Today still had three big advantages. The first was money. Its budget was at least five times bigger than ours. It had producers, reporters, a dedicated newsreader and a travelling weather presenter. It was a major production with major resources. We were a two-bit production run from an old tin shed. We didn't even have a proper set. Steven Claus and I used our own money to buy things like fake pot plants to make the studio look more homely.

Its second advantage was ratings. Even though we suspected many people had stopped watching *Today,* it still commanded an average audience of almost half a million people a day. We hadn't even cracked 90000.

In smaller markets like Adelaide, fewer than 10000 people were watching *Sunrise.* We knew that changing viewer behaviour wouldn't be easy, especially at breakfast. People had a routine. Even if they weren't sitting in front of the television, many had it on as background noise while getting ready for work. For twenty-one years, *Today* had provided that noise.

And, finally, *Today* had a supportive network. Nine prided itself on its supremacy in news and current affairs. *Today* was one of its flagship shows, and Steve and Tracy were network stars. Over at Seven, we knew we'd have Buckley's of getting promotion, and Kochie and Mel were anything but stars. One was a dorky finance nerd and the other was seen by some in the newsroom as a suburban mum without the shrewdness to survive television politics.

None of that put us off. We were on a mission and had the zeal of true believers. The new format kicked in at the start of December 2002.

Kochie quickly adapted to being himself on air. If anything, he was sharing *too* much. One morning he blurted out that he'd had an erection while sitting in front of his wife, Libby, at her parents' house, while her mum was on the adjoining couch. Mel struggled to retain her composure, but nearly cried from laughing. Libby wasn't laughing. She sent him a one-line text during the show: 'How dare you.' But viewers loved it. They loved Kochie's honesty and Mel's reaction to it. They emailed us by the minute to say so. Over the coming months, Kochie's mother-in-law often came up during on-air banter.

He always referred to her, lovingly, as 'The Dragon'. She was annoyed at first but came to embrace it after becoming a quasi-celebrity at her golf club.

Laughing soon became a staple of the show. None of it was forced and none of it was planned. That's why it worked. Everything on *Sunrise* just seemed so natural and so unlike our competitor. Our studio crew helped create the casual feel. 'During a news bulletin, you're meant to be a silent operator who doesn't react to anything,' says Paul Slater, one of our original cameramen. 'With *Sunrise,* the normal rules were thrown out the window. It was strange for us to now have a boss who got angry if we *didn't* react.'

But joking around wouldn't be enough to make us a credible alternative to *Today.* Our editorial agenda had to resonate in what we labelled 'heartland Australia'. We even had a typical viewer in mind: a woman in her early forties with a couple of kids, doing her best to afford the weekly grocery bill. We liked to call her 'Irene'. Whenever we considered stories, Matt Clarke and I would first ask, 'Would Irene give a shit?' I was strongly of the view that Irene was sick of politicians. They had a lot to say (usually on *Today)* but seemed out of touch with the everyday struggles of our viewers. I didn't see a reason to have them on the show. In fact, we all but banned them.

As supervising producer, Matt often had to cop the flak for my more controversial decisions; I just refused to pick up the phone. Our rejection of politicians caused him immeasurable grief in Canberra. Seven's bureau chief, Glenn Milne, led the backlash. 'At one stage,' recalls Matt, 'he told me we were idiots. When I explained that politicians didn't rate, he insisted we should be what he called a "loss leader (sacrificing ratings to keep politicians on side)". Our view was that we should be giving people what they want to watch, rather than what people in the newsroom *thought* they wanted to watch.'

And people *did* want to watch. Within three months of our new approach kicking in, our audience had climbed by more than thirty per cent.

But that wasn't enough to satisfy some of Seven's then programmers who were particularly peeved by my decision to have a new opening for the show: 'Now, from Brekky Central, this is *Sunrise* on Seven with Kochie and Mel.'

Brekky Central? Kochie? Mel?

'What the hell are you doing?' asked one. He insisted that by using 'silly phrases' like Brekky Central, I'd undermined the entire network's credibility. He also didn't accept that shortening the presenters' names made them sound down to earth. 'Their names are David Koch and Melissa Doyle. That's what I want to hear on air.' We played along for a while but encouraged our guests to call the hosts Kochie and

Mel. Ian Cook later told me he came under pressure to remove me due to what some considered my disregard for authority. Kerry Stokes's son, Ryan, may have unknowingly saved me, when he told a room full of Channel Seven executives that *Sunrise* had real potential.

***

The network still wasn't promoting us but we were creating noise in other ways. In early 2003, Kochie was talking about rugby union when he referred to a South African player as a 'boofhead'. Some people complained that he'd used language that should be kept off breakfast television.

The following morning, we tackled the subject of offensive language with Sue Butler from the Macquarie Dictionary. She was invited on by my former 4BC colleague Mark Dransfield, who I'd recruited as a *Sunrise* producer.

During his pre-show conversation with Sue, he told her, 'Of course, we won't have to use any swearwords on air.' But *she* heard, 'Of course, you can say any swearwords on air.' And, sure enough, she did.

> Butler: Today's taboos are all about labels that you use for people. So that the sentence 'You are a' is practically a no no. You cannot use...
>
> Kochie: Even if you use boofhead?

Butler: Even if you use boofhead because you're putting it in the same context as things which are clearly rude. You know, 'You are a fuckwit.' Well, obviously we know that's bad.

Control room producer David Walters started screaming in Kochie's and Mel's earpieces: 'Throw to a break! Throw to a break!'

Mel: Sue, we've run out of time but thanks so much for coming in. Big can of worms there.

You could say that again. Kochie and Mel tried to fix things after the break.

Mel: We must make a very quick apology. In our last interview, you might have heard a word used by our guest that we don't condone on this program so we wrapped the interview up relatively quickly as you might have noticed. We apologise to anyone who might have taken offence to that word. It's not one that will ever be repeated.

Rather than being offended, most of our viewers thought it was hilarious. In what was now true *Sunrise* style, we read their emails on air.

Kochie: This one says: 'Well done for handling the situation professionally, but the lady looked so prim and proper so it caught us by surprise too when she came out with that saying. I thought it was really funny.'

Our approach bemused the team at the ABC's *Media Watch.* Presenter David Marr labelled us nincompoops. Well, sort of.

> Marr: The gang at *Sunrise* could look up 'fuckwit' in Sue Butler's Macquarie Dictionary.

He then showed a graphic that revealed the word to mean nincompoop, implying it was an apt description of us.

We weren't even remotely insulted. It was national publicity for a breakfast show that was doing all it could to be noticed. It could only help our already growing ratings.

The thing that really made a difference, though, wasn't a free kick for us but an own goal from *Today.* Steve Liebmann was about to walk into a trap entirely of his making.

4

GIVE FEAR THE FLICK

Sixteen months had passed since the 9/11 attacks on America but many Australians were still living in fear. The Howard government talked about terrorism more than it talked about Medicare. In 2003, Steve Liebmann was recruited to be the poster boy for the so-called fight for freedom.

The veteran journalist was paid $55000 for a walk in the park—literally. Here's what he said while taking a stroll in a thirty-second government commercial:

> Terrorism has changed the world and Australia is not immune. Our security agencies have been upgraded and are ready to detect, prevent and respond to terrorism. All of us can play a part by keeping an eye out for anything suspicious. Be alert, but not alarmed. Together, let's look out for Australia.

The campaign coincided with the release of Michael Moore's documentary *Bowling for Columbine* that argued governments had used 9/11 to keep everyone on edge. That, said Moore, allowed them to increase their powers while decreasing civil liberties. Everything he said rang true. I walked out of the cinema after seeing the film and phoned *Sunrise* supervising producer Matt Clarke. 'I was at the beach on holidays and you called, speaking a million miles an hour,' says Matt. 'You wanted to run an on-air campaign telling everyone that everything is all right. There was no reason to worry.'

The *Campaign for Optimism* was born, with its dual taglines 'Give Fear the Flick' and 'Spread the Love'. Matt lined up guest after guest to put the threat in perspective. They revealed that Australians were 12000 times more likely to die from cancer than from terrorism; we spoke to psychologists who urged parents to stop frightening their kids. We even had bumper stickers printed. They, too, got us into trouble with the network because, apparently, the colour of the Channel Seven logo wasn't as red as it should have been. We were ordered to destroy however many were left. Even so, the stickers proved just as popular with viewers as a poem written by Brisbane's Robert Raftery.

> We've assembled like an anthem in one big, sharp, national prick, To punctuate terror's bubble and Give Fear the Flick.

> We've all had a guzzler's gutful, of all this terror talk, And I reckon it's time to settle down, and give the fear the fork, Just suck it in ... the majesty, as the Maker had intended, Let's refocus the fear, and re-engineer ... the Banjo's Vision Splendid.

And refocus, it did. We managed to portray Steve Liebmann as a government puppet without ever mentioning his name. The thing he valued the most—his credibility—was now in question. And he knew it. During an interview with the *Sydney Morning Herald,* he asked: 'Am I a crusader of credibility? Yes, you bet. Mine, the program's and I worry about it from time to time.' With good reason. Viewers emailed us to thank *Sunrise* for telling it how it was, rather than telling it how the government wanted us to think it was.

***

There are few people in television I respect more than Peter Meakin. A Walkley Award winner, he is the undisputed Godfather of news and current affairs in Australia. Like David Leckie, Meakin made his name at Channel Nine, as a provocative reporter, then mischief-making producer and, finally, the head of Nine's then unbeatable news machine. During his almost thirty years at Nine, Meakin was a key player in ensuring the network was 'still the one'.

That all came to an end in late February 2003, when Meakin had a falling-out with Nine's then chief executive, John Alexander. Actually, 'falling-out' is putting it lightly. Meakin called Kerry Packer to resign, famously telling him that Alexander was a 'twenty-four-carat cunt'.

Lack of subtlety is a Peter Meakin trademark. And so is his dishevelled appearance. After making the almost unthinkable switch to Channel Seven to become the head of news and current affairs, he walked into the *Sunrise* studio dressed in a white Bonds T-shirt and an old pair of baggy jeans. Kochie thought he was the new stagehand, so went to introduce himself: 'Hello, mate, welcome to the show. My name's David.' Our new boss responded: 'Yes, I know. My name's Peter Meakin.'

Meakin had an instant impact on the way *Sunrise*, and the news division in general, was treated. He says of Seven, 'It was different from Nine. There was more bureaucracy and layers of people who decided if something was a good or bad idea. The programming department had to be convinced that news and current affairs had any merit at all. There was a feeling at Seven that if a big news story happened, it shouldn't be promoted because it would only encourage people to watch Nine.'

Meakin had clout and, thankfully for me, he was a fan of *Sunrise.* That meant I had his support to get things done. The newsroom was now co-operating, albeit begrudgingly (one staffer referred to us as *Scumrise)* and the programmers started to butt out. Meakin was on hand for advice and firepower, but rarely interfered. Like Ian Cook before him, he was happy just to let us play.

54

And play we did. Movies, in particular, seemed to have far too big an influence on us. After seeing the Hugh Grant comedy *Love Actually,* we decided to take the entire show to Sydney Airport. Kochie, Mel and the rest of the team spent the morning broadcasting from the arrivals gate, in the hope that people, just like in the movie, would greet relatives and friends with hugs. What better way to *spread the love?* Of course, things are never like they are in the movies, though: during our broadcast, the only hugs on offer were from our reporter, Monique Wright, as she confronted love-shy business travellers.

Sunrise ratings were continuing to climb. In March 2003, Channel Seven commissioned David Castran, considered by many to be Australia's leading analyst of television trends, to research perceptions of its nightly news service in regional Queensland. But viewers wanted to talk about something else. 'They just kept spontaneously bringing up *Sunrise,*' he remembers. 'There was a lot of chatter in our focus groups. People would say things like "It's fresh", and described Kochie and Mel as "normal" and less formal than Channel Nine's breakfast team.' For us, being 'normal' was a badge of honour. It was also a damning indictment of television generally that viewers saw other hosts as anything but. As Kochie put it: 'This is quite a wanky industry. It's all about image and trying to convey an image that's manufactured, rather than being a normal person.' I think Kochie's wife, Libby, had much to do with keeping him grounded. She couldn't have cared less about ratings or the apparent glamour of television. She always made sure that family remained his priority.

Regional Queensland was the first to switch to *Sunrise* en masse. Lifestyle played a part—viewers tended to get out of bed earlier there than in other places. But they also felt a connection with Kochie and Mel, who they saw as *their* type of people: down to earth and without big egos. Kochie was genuinely surprised when organisers of the Cairns Jazz Festival approached him to be their master of ceremonies in 2003. He'd only ever been asked to host finance events. The night before the festival, Kochie and Libby were walking along the Cairns Esplanade when locals started calling out at him about *Sunrise:* 'Love the show, mate.' 'Say g'day to Mel.' 'Keep giving those pollies hell.' Two women even asked him for a hug. He turned to Libby and said, 'Holy shit. Something's happening up here.'

By the end of April 2003, it was happening across Australia. Our ratings kept climbing. The spikes shown in regional Queensland were now duplicated in bigger markets, like Brisbane and Melbourne. That was made even more remarkable by the fact that we weren't getting any significant promotion from Channel Seven. And that takes us to the heart of why *Sunrise* worked as quickly as it did. By creating a conversation with our audience, we also generated an active word-of-mouth campaign. This campaign operated in many ways.

One of the most successful was when we asked viewers to nominate their favourite butcher or café, as part of our commitment to support small business. They responded in big numbers: cafés across Australia switched their televisions to *Sunrise,* butchers told their customers about the show while seeking nominations. Kochie also started to read out jokes every day, most provided by viewers (who loved hearing their names on television). Many of those jokes went viral. Every time someone emailed a joke around, the profile of our show got bigger. And then there was perhaps our best weapon of all: a simple whiteboard. We called it the ROSwall. At face value, 'ROS' stood for 'Responses of Sunrisers' but it was also a subtle dig at one-time federal sports minister Ros Kelly, who'd raised eyebrows by revealing she allocated grants with 'a great big whiteboard'.

The ROSwall became an icon of the show; it would sit on set as a permanent reminder that *Sunrise* belonged to our viewers. People could email us with things they wanted discussed, or problems they wanted fixed, be it an intersection without lights or a council overcharging ratepayers. We'd then write it on the whiteboard, where it would stay until we delivered. The ROSwall proved so popular that we had to assign a full-time producer just to sift through our emails. Who needed technology? We had a whiteboard.

The engagement with our audience created the kind of buzz that social media does today, but without the cynicism and negativity. (These days, David Koch stays off Twitter during the show.) It connected us with our viewers, and our viewers with each other. We later exploited that further by creating the *Sunrise* Family Loyalty Club and almost half a million people applied to be card-carrying members. No other show or media company could boast anything like it.

Some Seven executives still struggled to understand our appeal and labelled our family 'the Mansons'. 'I suggested they could have called us the Partridge family rather than the Mansons,' joked Kochie, 'but I think it's been bred out of adversity.'

The family was about to get a powerful new member with the arrival of our new chief executive. Like Peter Meakin, David Leckie was determined to change Seven's culture. 'Leckie wanted to win,' says Peter Meakin. 'Leckie wanted to win across the board. His feeling was that if we weren't number one in news, we might as well close down the news division. I don't think he ever meant it, but it was a good opening statement to get people's attention.'

I loved everything about David Leckie. I loved his swearing; I loved his arrogance (which, across the years, I discovered to be little more than bravado used to overcome deep insecurities); I loved his ability to make things happen; and, most of all, I loved the faith he placed in a little show being produced from an old tin shed. He felt the values of *Sunrise* should represent those of Seven itself. Leckie told his executive team to stop pretending to be Channel Nine.

'I looked at *Sunrise* and said, "Right, that's what we should be,"' is how he described it to the *Sydney Morning Herald* in 2008.

As happy as I was with our ratings and rising stocks internally, I also knew that Chris Reason, who was winning his battle with cancer, would never return to the show. The success of both the format and David Koch had made sure of that. (Reaso would later host Seven's mid-morning news bulletin that, by his own admission, better suited his style.) With Kochie now locked in, the uncertainty shifted to Mel. I feared our momentum could come to a halt when, in May 2003, she told me she was pregnant. Selfish of me, I know, but my sole focus was on beating *Today,* something considered farcical just six months earlier. But, rather than slow us down, the pregnancy was a boon. By then, Mel had become much more comfortable talking about herself. And it was just as well because viewers couldn't get enough. She told our audience she didn't know whether she was expecting a boy or girl but that her young son, Nick, had dubbed it 'Noodles' after his favourite food. Soon she was overwhelmed by viewers' cards and gifts, which even included knitted blankets. It was hard to imagine viewers doing that for anyone else on television.

They became just as familiar with Kochie's family (and not only The Dragon). In late 2003 his son AJ was among the so-called schoolies celebrating on the Gold Coast, and Kochie thought it would be a good idea to call him during the show for a live on-the-spot report. Problem was, AJ wasn't the one who answered.

'Hello, this is AJ's phone,' said the young female voice on the other end of the line.

'Oh, who's this?' asked a slightly startled Kochie.

'This is Candy. AJ's just in the shower.'

Kochie was clearly thinking *Oh, fuck,* while the studio crew (and, no doubt, many watching from home) burst out laughing. Mel left him hanging out to dry for a minute or two before revealing he'd been set up. The female voice actually belonged to one of our producers back in the office.

The stunt was the idea of our line producer, David 'Dougie' Walters, whose role in the rise of *Sunrise* deserves recognition. I met Dougie in the newsroom, where he wrote finance reports. Just from chatting to him, it was obvious he was capable of more. He was smart, quick-witted and versatile. As with Mark Dransfield and myself, his background was radio. For me, that sealed the deal: I wanted him on our team. Back in 2003, most people working in television news were accustomed to just one deadline a day. That was a different world from radio, where journos churned out copy every hour, on the hour. I wanted radio's sense of immediacy to be part of everything *Sunrise* did—be it covering breaking news or pulling a last-minute joke on David Koch. Dougie made that happen.

Someone else who'd mastered the art of humour was a young reporter working on Channel Ten's Sydney news. His name was Grant Denyer. I first noticed him while he was covering Sydney's Royal Easter Show (a job usually assigned to the most junior reporter). He made the story his own. Instead of just talking about skateboard stunt riders, he adopted their lingo. Instead of just interviewing kids, he went with them on rides. At just under 165 centimetres tall, Grant was a pocket-sized bundle of cuteness. There was no question he had the makings of a star. He had obvious appeal to what some in the industry liked to call the three Gs: Girls, Gays and Grannies. He also had appeal to the *Sunrise* production team; we'd cheer whenever he came on the telly. What a talent, we thought. And what a waste for him to be doing ninety-second reports on a news service.

I called Grant one night while I was walking home from work (I never liked to live far from the studio) and invited him to join the show as our weatherman. He told me that that wasn't something he knew much about, but I assured him the job was so much more. If he wanted to jump from a plane, he could. If he wanted to swim with sharks, that was fine. He had free rein to show Australia who he really was. More importantly for Grant, he had free rein to show Australia to Australia. He'd grown up on a farm and always felt more at home in the country. Here was the chance to spend more time there, while still being seen in the big smoke. David Leckie suggested we offer him a ute to get him to Seven. That wasn't necessary. Grant soon realised he'd been offered his dream gig and became our weather guy. In true *Sunrise* style, we introduced him without much fanfare or slick network commercials. In fact, we made a promo using little more than a garden hose. Grant stood under what we tried to pass off as rain, while another *Sunrise* staffer offered him an umbrella. He was then heard to respond, 'No thanks, I'm the weather guy.' Saatchi & Saatchi, eat your heart out.

Grant joined not just Kochie and Mel but newsreader Natalie Barr and sports presenter Mark Beretta. Beretts, as he was better known, was someone I'd worked with on the original *Sunrise* bulletin. When his tenure reading sport at 6pm came to an end, I wanted him back on the show. Just like the others on the team, he was firmly in touch with everyday Australia. He was born in working-class Geelong, and had strong bonds to family and sport (including his beloved Geelong AFL team). He also liked to waterski and had won a national title at the age of fourteen. Beretts had humour but also humility. I remember watching him get choked up while running with the Olympic torch in 2000. He said that sharing the experience with his family was the thing he was most proud of.

Natalie Barr hailed from Bunbury, a relatively small city in Western Australia, and was never going to stick around. In next to no time, she was working for a TV station in Los Angeles. She was good. So good that she was nominated for a major award for her coverage of the OJ Simpson car chase. While Mel Doyle's the kind of person who brings you soup when you're sick, Nat's the one who tells you to just get over it. She's not mean, just direct, and is never afraid to share her true feelings (she caused a storm fairly recently, by telling women to stop blaming men for their troubles). She also has a somewhat warped a sense of humour (she once cracked up on air while reporting on two women who tried to take their dead relative on a flight) and a cheeky persona. One executive liked to call her 'the naughty school mum'.

One member of the team would go on to become a network star by simply entering a competition. When Edwina Bartholomew was studying journalism in Bathurst she, like any uni student, rarely got out of bed before 11am. Fortunately, her lecturer did, and told her that *Sunrise* was looking for a junior producer via a competition called 'The Intern'—which was basically a rip-off of *The Apprentice.* Edwina was one of ten people who competed in a series of tasks before one got 'sacked' each day on air. But, just a few days in, viewers made it clear they hated the segment, considering it to be cruel and unsuitable for a breakfast show committed to spreading the love. We axed the competition without ever finding a winner.

Two candidates, however, impressed us from day one, so we hired them both. The first was David Robinson, who is now a producer on Channel Ten's morning show, *Studio 10.* The other was Edwina. Businesslike, she'd turn up each day, with a list of story ideas and even with presentations on how to make *Sunrise* better (not bad for someone who'd never watched the show). She took everything so seriously that when she arrived one morning with a security tag sticking out of her knickers, she almost fainted (she assured us she did actually pay for them). Before long, she became our ROSwall researcher, with the job of getting the answers for our viewers to be given on air. Anyone who encountered her in those early days knew she'd go far, and she's now the *Sunrise* weather presenter and co-host of *Dancing with the Stars.* Edwina could easily do just about any job in television, including, if she chose, that of executive producer.

Getting a presenting line-up right is all about balance. While those in the cast need to like each other, they can't be clones of each other. They should have different interests, different passions and different views. The common thread in our team was that no one pretended to be someone they weren't. As Alice Gorman wrote in the *Gold Coast Bulletin: 'Sunrise* works because the set is an ego-free zone. Well, that's how it comes across anyway. Either these guys are really great actors or they really like each other.' They really *did* like each other. So much so that a body language expert in Queensland speculated that Kochie and Mel were having an affair. They weren't, but they did refer to each other as 'partner' off air.

We ended 2003 within striking distance of *Today.* Our ratings had climbed to 227000, while our opponents

64

plunged to 246000. It was a spectacular turnaround that rattled Nine.

Long-time executive producer of *Toda* y Steve Wood was replaced by Darren Wick, who'd earned his stripes in the rough and tumble world of tabloid television, on Nine's *A Current Affair.* Wick felt *Today* had become complacent, and was determined to do whatever it took to get the show back on track. That included threatening to ban from his show people who dared to appear on *Sunrise* (as I will talk about later, I did a very similar thing five years afterwards, with entertainment companies). I sent Wick a blunt email accusing him of standover tactics. He fired back: 'Get used to the real world, little boy. Your honeymoon is over.'

***

When I wasn't at Channel Seven, I was usually asleep. Working the type of hours I did meant I rarely went out to bars or clubs, which didn't bother me, as I was too socially awkward to visit them anyway. It was perhaps no surprise then that I found love at work.

Yoko Shimizu was a producer in the Seven newsroom when I invited her to join *Sunrise.* She didn't accept the offer straightaway, fearing we were too far removed from what she considered serious news, but Kochie convinced her that she wouldn't regret embarking on the *Sunrise* adventure. It didn't take long for Yoko and me to become close. I didn't just like her for her mind; her laugh was one of the loudest I'd ever heard. As well as our developing personal relationship, she had a major influence on the way I did my job. She was the one who held me back from jumping the shark. She knew when my ideas were just too nutty and was always happy to tell me so. She also told me when they were good and encouraged me to make them better. I came to depend on Yoko to bring order to my otherwise chaotic mind.

But, as she told the *Sydney Morning Herald* in 2008, I wasn't the easiest of boyfriends to live with. 'It used to frustrate the hell out of me that any free time we had, he would spend in front of the computer coming up with new ideas for the show.' Dinners at home sometimes resembled production meetings, as Yoko and I lived with fellow *Sunrise* staffers Mark Dransfield and Steven Claus. Mark dubbed it the 'House of the Rising Sun'.

And rising we were. On 8 February 2004, for the first time *Sunrise* overtook *Today* in national ratings. The margin wasn't big—just on 9000 viewers—but that mattered little. We'd secured a win with a format that was just over a year old. It was a day everyone who was then at *Sunrise* remembers. We had what for us was a major celebration at the local pub (though we needed to be home in bed by 7pm).

Kerry Stokes was just as happy. He invited the presenters and me to lunch at his waterfront property in Sydney's eastern suburbs. We were all nervous as hell, and clearly a long way from our tin shed, when a butler greeted us at the door and asked to take our coats. I gave him my jumper. Lunch was in Stokes's backyard, but perhaps that's not the right term for what looked more like a bowling green that stretched all the way to the harbour. Proud *Sunrise* viewer Ryan Stokes pointed out some Sydney landmarks, in what always struck me as his nervous American twang; he is immensely likeable and never pretends to know more than anyone else. Kochie, not unfamiliar with titans of business, led most of the lunchtime conversation, while the rest of us tried our best to look comfortable. Stokes Senior praised the show, while instructing us to maintain the pressure on Nine: 'We've waited a long time for this.'

Veteran Nine producer Gerald Stone wrote in *Who Killed Channel 9?*: '*Today'* s loss to *Sunrise* may have been out of primetime, but its psychological impact was considerable.' This wasn't just at Nine. It gave many at Seven renewed confidence that we could win across the board. Nine did all it could to reclaim lost ground but its producers were clearly on the ropes when they started to copy *Sunrise* innovations.

We introduced Australia's first permanent news ticker (the moving bar showing headlines at the bottom of the screen) because I felt it suited breakfast viewing behaviour in which people tend to tune in for only short periods of time while getting dressed or buttering toast. A ticker would allow them to get news when they wanted, rather than needing to wait around for scheduled updates on the half-hour. Just months later (and having been without one for two decades), *Today* launched one of its own. More tellingly, Darren Wick pushed his team to take a more informal approach. Steve Liebmann plainly wasn't happy, looking uncomfortable every time he stepped out from behind the desk. (He'd later tell the *Age* that *Today* 'had become a poor imitation of *Sunrise*'.)

The final nail in *Today's* coffin came in August 2004 with Seven's move to the heart of Sydney and to something almost impossible for any other station to replicate. Our new home was a big glass studio on busy Martin Place. Anyone could now watch *Sunrise* being made and chat with the team up close. For a show that prided itself on viewer interaction, living in a fishbowl was a dream come true (I insisted we keep using the term 'shed' to describe our new production office, as a reminder of where we started.)

From the moment we moved to Martin Place, nobody could doubt that *Sunrise* was Australia's most watched breakfast show. We won every day and every week. The once untouchable *Today* was lost somewhere in our wake. Papers labelled it Nine's 'cereal disaster'.

But, for me, that wasn't enough.

I wanted our ratings to climb even further and so gave my team a challenge. Level 41 was one of

Sydney's top restaurants. As its name suggested, it sat high above the city—which was apt, I thought, for a show still looking towards the sky. I promised to take the entire team there as soon as we had 400000 viewers (we'd recently passed the milestone of 300000).

My determination wasn't just fuelled by competition with Nine (and, in particular, Darren Wick) but by an internal vendetta. I wanted to humble those who'd doubted we could win—the ones who referred to us as *Scumrise* or the Mansons. Writing for Fairfax newspapers, Jane Cadzow observed I had a 'capacity for slow steady hatred' that scared many of my colleagues. This probably wasn't helped when they saw me hurl my BlackBerry or kick a chair. Even the slightest things made me lose my cool, such was my obsession to make the show perfect. It didn't scare those in my inner circle. We were extremely close-knit, which perhaps contributed to notions that we resembled a cult. But Cadzow was right about the intensity with which I could hold a grudge (I like to think it's a character flaw I have since overcome).

I wanted to prove we weren't just an overnight sensation. And the job of doing that was anything but done.

5

POLLIE POWER

Sunrise was never afraid to take the piss out of pollies, but David Koch took that to a new level in 2004. There was hell to pay after he read out one viewer's joke on air.

Kochie: John Howard is on a skiing trip—Christmas holidays, Aspen, the whole thing. He's coming down the slopes when he notices someone has obviously relieved themselves in the show and written 'John Howard is a dork'.

Well, John stops in front of it and looked at it absolutely fuming and says to his federal police guys who are shadowing him: 'Look into this. I want to know who did it and under what circumstances.' The forensic guys took some samples.

Later that night, they had the results.

'Well, Mr Prime Minister, we've got good news and bad news. We've tested the urine samples and we've come to a conclusion. Would you like the good or bad news first?'

And John says, 'Well, what's the good news?'

And they said, 'It's Kim Beazley's urine.'

And he said, 'Well, what's the bad news?'

They replied, 'It was in Janette's handwriting.'

The joke wasn't original. It had been around for years, but usually featured Bill and Hillary Clinton; swapping them for the Howards was always going to cause a backlash. Kochie got a sense of that as soon as he reached the punchline. There was an awkward laugh from Natalie Barr, who was filling in for Mel, before she asked, 'Did you vet that with anyone?'

He hadn't.

Viewer complaints flooded in. Towards the end of the show, Kochie got defensive: 'It's a joke. That's what we are talking about. We are not talking about the state of the nation or climate change or anything like that. It's a joke.'

Kochie had a tendency to offend people from time to time, be they politicians, advertisers, viewers or executives. It was my job to shield him from most of their objections. His value to *Sunrise* depended on him having the freedom to be himself and not needing to walk on eggshells. That's not to say he was given a totally free rein. It was also my job to pull him back when it was needed—something he trusted me to do. But on this occasion, there was little I could do to put out the fire.

Kerry Stokes personally instructed Kochie to write a letter of apology to the prime minister and his wife. Kochie still couldn't understand what all the fuss was about but was wise enough to avoid arguing with our proprietor. To this day, John Howard refuses to talk to Kochie, even when seated on the same table at functions. I suspect the joke is only part of the reason. The former prime minister is only too aware of the role *Sunrise* played in the rise of Kevin Rudd.

***

By 2004, Rudd had been appearing on the show for almost eighteen months. We'd decided to relax our ban on political interviews, so that our viewers would feel they had direct access to decision makers. We saw it as an extension of the *Sunrise* philosophy of getting things done. But that meant we had a very different approach from other programs to when and why politicians would appear.

We opted to find two frontbenchers, one from each side of politics, to become regulars on the show. The same pairing would be required every Friday morning for what we described as their weekly appointment with the electorate. The rules were simple: they'd need to answer anything we asked, even if it fell outside their portfolios (and it usually did). Many of the questions would come from our viewers; some would have featured on the ROSwall. Spin and waffle were banned. If Kochie and Mel heard anything that resembled pollie speak, they'd cut the conversation short. Answers had to be brief and honest.

Small business minister Joe Hockey and shadow foreign minister Kevin Rudd agreed to take part (both men were on the rise and keen to be noticed) but Rudd had some concerns about keeping his answers short. 'Kevin said to me, "I can't say anything meaningful in 20 seconds,"' recalls Matt Clarke. 'So I said, "Why don't we try it? I'll ask you a question and put the stopwatch on and I'll tell you when twenty seconds is up." I asked him the question. He talked and finished. And then he said, "I told you I couldn't do that in twenty seconds." I said, "You're right, Kevin, that was only seventeen."'

Rudd and Hockey adapted to our format and, in doing so, made politics accessible to middle Australia. The payoff for them was enormous: a new audience that normally tuned out when politicians opened their mouths. A few months after starting with the show, Joe Hockey was on a ministerial visit to Coober Pedy. A miner approached him and said, 'I know you. You're that bloke on *Sunrise.*'

'Joe and Kevin gave of themselves,' says Peter Meakin. 'They clearly seemed to like each other and the audience responded by giving them brownie points for appearing to be non-politicians, even though they were in fact playing politics all along. They were just playing it smart.'

I'm not as cynical as Meakin. Both men knew the segment played well in the electorate, but I think it also disarmed them. They enjoyed just being themselves without having to stick to the day's pre-defined talking points or take pot shots for the sake of it. Alister Jordan was Kevin Rudd's chief of staff. He tells me: 'You got to see more of the real Kevin in those interviews than you did in many other media forums. The format didn't allow either Kevin or Joe to be politicians.'

After each show, Rudd, Hockey and Jordan would have breakfast together at Bond Café, alongside the *Sunrise* studio on Phillip Street. The staff kept watch on the telly and knew to start preparing their orders (the same each week) as soon as their segment was wrapping up. Rudd and Hockey's blossoming friendship unnerved some in the Howard government. Until *Sunrise,* Kevin Rudd's ambitions weren't considered threatening. Members on both sides of the House felt voters saw him as nothing more than an awkward-looking nerd without the X factor required to be leader. In his memoir, Peter Costello wrote: 'Hockey may have helped Rudd's rise by appearing to make him look more human, less ambitious and driven.'

The segment wasn't just about style; the substance came with their active involvement in *Sunrise* causes.

There was perhaps none bigger than a campaign we called 'Cool the Globe'. Both Rudd and Hockey told our viewers that they accepted the science around climate change. So much so that Hockey even signed a *Sunrise* petition calling on the government of which he was a member to keep a rebate on solar energy. Faced with 170000 signatures, including the one from his fellow minister, Peter Costello came on the show to announce the rebate would stay. 'Well done and congratulations to you,' said the treasurer.

I never had any hesitation in pushing our activism to the limit. What's the point of having a platform if you don't use it? Not only did *Sunrise* partner with the Australian Conservation Foundation to run weekly workshops on making homes green-friendly, but Kochie and Mel both took part in the protest march 'Walk Against Warming' (in fact, Mel hosted the Sydney event). And we matched words with action, by commissioning an emissions audit of Seven's Martin Place headquarters. The government's Greenhouse Office declared *Sunrise* to be the first carbon-neutral show on Australian television, much to the chagrin of right-wing columnist Andrew Bolt: 'Being carbon neutral shouldn't be hard for a TV program that produces only hot air.'

Those kinds of cheap shots didn't scare Rudd or Hockey away; our viewership was just too powerful. And, to some extent, they became part of the family. I once turned up for a party at Kochie's house to see a government car and driver out the front. Inside, I had a drink with Kevin, while he told me (as he did most people) of his plan to be leader. Joe and Kevin even agreed to be in a *Sunrise* music clip. As part of our continuing crusade to 'Give Fear the Flick', the *Sunrise* team performed a version of 'Where is the Love?' by American hip-hop group the Black Eyed Peas (we discovered that Kochie and Mel weren't the best of singers).

> The frontbenchers tried their best to rap their lines.
>
> Rudd: That's the reason sometimes I'm feeling under.
>
> Hockey: That's the reason I'm sometimes feeling down.
>
> Rudd: There's no wonder I'm sometimes feeling under.
>
> Hockey: Gotta keep my faith alive until the love is found.

Their duet ended with them shoulder to shoulder, attempting what I think was some form of rapper hand gesture. The performance was daggy, unforgettable and hilarious.

Rudd and Hockey's weekly segments proved that our leaders could rise above adversarial politics and that credibility wouldn't suffer as a result. Best of all, we'd found a way to make politicians rate. 'It was a masterstroke. It transformed two careers and was one of the golden moments of Channel Seven,' says Meakin. 'One guy went on to become prime minister and the other is now federal treasurer, and both of them were infinitely more interesting people to the electorate as a result of appearing on *Sunrise.*'

6

REACHING OUT TO ASIA

Music blaring. Producers debating. A manic boss shouting out ideas. It was rare for the *Sunrise* production office to fall silent. But it happened on the morning of Monday, 27 December 2004, as pictures came in from southern Asia.

We'd heard about an earthquake and tsunami the day before: a news update during the Boxing Day cricket test reported that a few hundred people might be dead. Later that day, radio stations were interviewing Australian tourists in Thailand, who described widespread destruction. Now, we were seeing it for ourselves. *Sunrise* producers sat around our wall of six monitors, as raw video feeds came in from across the region. The most upsetting pictures that day were from Sri Lanka. We watched as people clung desperately to poles while their towns were invaded by seawater. You could hear them scream when they saw friends and relatives succumb to the current. By Wednesday, home video from tourists in Thailand emerged. It showed the moment the wave hit and its undeniable force; those in its path were slammed into trees and dragged underwater. It was easy to see why the death toll was rising so quickly: 20000 yesterday, 80000 today. It would surely hit 100000 by the weekend.

Yoko and I were due to fly out on New Year's Day for a fortnight-long holiday in Europe. We both knew we'd need to postpone it. This wasn't a matter of doubting the team's ability to cover the story without us, it was that we knew *Sunrise* needed to do more than just report. David Koch used to say to me that our show wasn't 'Sydney TV'. By that, he meant that our priorities extended beyond rating points and spouting shallow slogans in promos (television stations love making commercials full of buzz words like 'trust' and 'experience'). We admired local stations in places like Perth that worked hard to both serve and inspire their communities with initiatives such as telethons. It was time for us to do the same. As soon as we came off air on Thursday, 30 December, I called a special production meeting and cancelled all leave. We'd need our entire team to help do the impossible.

Seven's programming department had agreed to *Sunrise* hosting a primetime concert on the steps of the Sydney Opera House on Saturday, 8 January—just nine days away. It was a tough deadline, but the concert would be a ticketed event with all proceeds going to relief efforts, and I felt we'd raise the most money while Australians were still coming to terms with the extent of human suffering the tsunami had caused. It wasn't the first time *Sunrise* had organised a concert: performers were used to dropping in on the show, but we'd never done anything with multiple artists at once or produced one in primetime. I knew this could put the show front and centre.

World Vision quickly agreed to be our partnering charity but securing the venue would prove more of a challenge. Seven's Dave Masala and I managed to get a meeting with the Opera House's management team on Friday morning who were incredulous at our plans: 'Today is New Year's Eve!' said one executive, as if Masala and I had somehow overlooked this. 'I don't think you have any understanding of what you're proposing.' We did, but sat silently. 'Most of our key personnel are on holiday. We have performances in the House that weekend. There are security and safety concerns. I think it's unreasonable of you to expect us to just throw this together in a week.'

This last point pushed me to the edge. 'Unreasonable?' I asked. 'Well, look, I'm sorry to be such a bother.' Masala had heard that sarcastic tone from me before and knew I was about to let loose. 'I might just call the hundreds of thousands of people who are without a home right now to tell them it's unreasonable to expect help.'

Guilt trips tend to work. They told us it was possible, providing we did most of the legwork. That meant organising everything from staging to crowd control to cleaning.

'Deal,' I said, as Masala cleared his throat.

Dave Masala is a loveable teddy and the only person I know who actually *did* get his career start in the mailroom. Thirty-four years later, there wasn't much he didn't know about television. He had a broad operations role at Seven's news headquarters, but I tended to monopolise him for *Sunrise.* He preferred this, because *Sunrise* projects were always more of a challenge than those of *Seven News* or *Today Tonight.* I'd never seen Dave show any signs of stress, no matter what I threw at him. As we walked back to Martin Place from the Opera House, he maintained a smile while pointing out I'd just agreed that he would almost single-handedly organise facilities and crewing at a time when most of our suppliers were closed. I asked whether he was cool with that. 'Of course,' he replied in his laconic way. And that's why I love him.

Later that day, I placed a call to Lesley Diskin from Ticketmaster, who was getting ready to go out for New Year's Eve. I told her we'd be announcing a concert during our show on Monday and were keen to open ticket sales for it at the same time. She didn't need to think twice but did need some basic details, like the cost of tickets.

'Um, what do you think is fair?' I asked.

'Well, it depends who's performing. Who are the headline acts?' was her obvious response.

'Um, let me get back to you.'

Yoko had started calling the major record companies and artists' managers while Dave and I were negotiating the venue. They all loved the idea but urged her to be realistic; many acts were locked into tours or on an end-of-year break. Luckily, Yoko was also good at guilt trips but, unlike mine, hers never offended. They all told her to give them twenty-four hours.

On New Year's Day, the aftermath of the tsunami was the only news that mattered. Ten Australians were confirmed dead but we all knew that toll would rise. The devastation was beyond belief. One man seeing it up close was our music reporter, the legendary Ian 'Molly' Meldrum. He'd been on a plane from Melbourne to Bangkok when the tsunami hit; he often spent Christmas in Australia before heading to Thailand to see in the new year. Molly, nearly in tears, called the *Sunrise* office from Phuket. One of his close friends had lost two of his brothers. He suggested we ask Yael Cohn to help us lock in performers. Yael was the person who made sure Molly got from point A to point B—he could be absent-minded at times, so she was there to fill in the blanks. That also meant she had close relationships with a who's who of Australian music. 'I was at a dance party in Melbourne when you called,' recalls Yael. 'You told me to just get on a plane. I walked into the *Sunrise* office on Sunday morning and I remember the place was just abuzz.'

By lunchtime on Sunday, the problem of not having any performers had turned into the problem of having too many. Managers were now calling *us* trying to get their acts on the bill, showing how deeply Australians had connected to the tragedy. Yoko and Yael were working with a whiteboard in the *Sunrise* conference room. They just kept adding names to it—Killing Heidi, Anthony Callea, Casey Donovan, Eskimo Joe, Marina Prior, The Whitlams and Thirsty Merc.

Talent agents told us that Channel Nine was also thinking of running an appeal of some kind, most likely during an upcoming cricket match. That gave us an idea—one that would create Australian television history.

David Leckie and I spoke on Sunday afternoon about expanding our concert to be a joint television event between the three commercial networks. We didn't know how something like that would work, but Leckie deserves significant credit for making it his crusade. By Monday, he'd won agreement from David Gyngell at Nine and John McAlpine at Ten for our concert to become a co-production. It would be televised on all three channels, commercial-free.

The network bosses issued a joint statement on Sunday, 2 January:

> Given the magnitude of the tsunami disaster, it's appropriate that the Australian television industry gets together in a non-partisan way to raise a substantial amount of money for the victims of this tragedy.

Free TV reaches virtually every person in Australia and it's only right that we harness our collective strengths to support the relief agencies' heroic efforts.

To underline the united approach, network ratings would be suspended for the night. We'd know the total audience but would never know who watched which station. Competition between the networks was hereby suspended. In theory.

Three executive producers were appointed to control the broadcast, one from each network. *Rove* producer Craig Campbell was put forward by Ten, *The Footy Show's* Glenn Pallister by Nine, and I would represent Seven. We had a meeting at the Channel Seven boardroom in Martin Place, and each of us brought a posse of publicists, promo producers and other random people whose only job was to make each network look stronger than the others. Pallister also brought his boss, Nine's director of production, Andrew Backwell.

It soon became clear that each network wanted to plant as many of its own stars in the broadcast as possible. Campbell proposed a solution: we'd go ahead with the concert in Sydney but run it in tandem with a telethon in Melbourne. We'd simply switch between both events all night. Given their very nature, telethons need as many celebrities as they can get. Famous faces take turns answering phones and doing silly stunts in exchange for donations, and you can always count on a heartthrob soapie star stripping down by the end of the night. Campbell's plan made a lot of sense.

So, who'd be in charge of what?

Campbell and I were quick to claim our turf. I'd take care of the Opera House concert and he'd be responsible for the Melbourne telethon. Campbell was from Melbourne and well versed in staging major events. That left Nine. Pallister offered to take an umbrella approach and serve as an intermediary. On the night, he'd be responsible for switching between the concert in Sydney and the telethon in Melbourne, to ensure one seamless broadcast.

The next question was who would host. Pallister suggested three hosts in Sydney and three in Melbourne. In other words, one from each network in both cities. I insisted I wouldn't separate Kochie and Mel in Sydney, arguing that viewers actually saw them as one person. Yes, it was a rather tenuous argument, but I was happy to run with it. This had started as a *Sunrise* event and I wasn't prepared to surrender having a level of ownership over the Sydney component, especially in primetime. I wanted Kochie and Mel upfront and together.

Campbell understood. I suspect Pallister would have agreed too, had it not been for Backwell, who was having none of it. He believed that having two hosts from Seven would defeat the entire spirit of the night—it was either a joint production or it wasn't.

He was right, of course, but that wasn't going to change my position. We went backward and forward for at least ten minutes before Campbell intervened. He was like a teacher who'd discovered two kids fighting in a sandpit. 'This should be above network politics,' he reminded us. He suggested Seven and Nine have two hosts each at the Opera House; he was even prepared to go with just one from Ten. Hard to say no to that.

The Sydney component would be hosted by David Koch and Melissa Doyle from Seven, Larry Emdur and Richard Wilkins from Nine, and Gretel Killeen from Ten. The telethon in Melbourne would be steered by Seven's Andrew O'Keefe, Nine's Eddie McGuire and Ten's Rove McManus. As Rove would later quip, 'Finally, Eddie McGuire on all three networks.'

My team had very little to do with the production in Melbourne. We assigned some senior Seven staffers to liaise with Campbell, but we all had faith in his ability to deliver. Pallister and his people at Nine went to work on the running order for the night. They needed to strike a tricky balance between Sydney and Melbourne, while also integrating live crosses from some of the worst-affected regions. The three networks had pooled satellite and reporter resources across Asia.

Back in the *Sunrise* production office, the phones were ringing off the hook. Companies from all over Sydney wanted to know how they could help, and soon everything from broadcast trucks to audio gear had been donated. We still faced our biggest challenge of all: deciding who'd get to perform in what was shaping up to be one of Australian television's most-watched concerts. There was no shortage of options—the whiteboard was covered in names; and more were being added. Agents were lobbying Yoko, Yael, and *Rove's* music producer, Anne Haebich, who'd joined us in Sydney. The problem was, we needed to cut, not add. We had less airtime than originally planned because we had to factor in the Melbourne component. Also, we weren't planning a routine Carols by Candlelight kind of night. We intended to put our audience on an emotional rollercoaster, with bursts of high energy interrupted by guaranteed tearjerkers. Getting the mix right wouldn't just guarantee a better concert but inspire more people to give.

We wanted a big opening but were in two minds about what that should be. Given the nature of the event, should we start with something reflective or get the crowd revved up immediately? The broadcast itself would be called *Australia Unites:Reach Out to Asia,* and Yael casually mentioned that it was a shame eighties rock band Noiseworks wasn't still around. Their hit song 'Touch' included the refrain 'Reach out and touch somebody'. As it happened, the band's manager, Michael Browning, was David Koch's brother-in-law. Just hours after Kochie extended an invite, the band was locked in; Noiseworks would reunite. That made our decision pretty simple. Their return to the stage would be our high profile, high-energy opening act.

If only the rest had been as easy.

Guy Sebastian and Anthony Callea both wanted to perform in Sydney, but we felt having two stars from *Australian Idol* would undermine the line-up's strength. To me, the choice was obvious. It had to be Callea. His single 'The Prayer', first made famous by Céline Dion and Andrea Bocelli, had just debuted on the Australian music charts at number one, and would set the perfect emotional tone. Yoko fought hard against this. She felt Sebastian was the stronger and more credible performer, and also pointed out that he had a personal link to the story. Sebastian was born in Malaysia—one of twelve Asian countries hit hard by the tsunami. I surrendered. Callea would be relegated to the Melbourne phone room. Sebastian was keen to sing 'Climb Every Mountain' but Craig Campbell feared the song could offend, given many people had died while trying to reach higher ground. Sebastian was insistent and called Yoko personally to make his case. He told her the song meant a great deal to him and promised we wouldn't regret it if he sang it. I gave him the green light.

Missy Higgins also made the cut in Sydney but, like Sebastian, there was some angst over song choice. We were keen for her to perform her massive hit 'Scar', which was the most played song on Australian radio at the time. Missy and her manager, John

Watson, pushed instead for something called 'The Special Two'—a song they weren't planning to release for some months. As soon as we heard it, we relented; it was one of those songs that lured you into self-reflection.

The act that would generate the most buzz leading into Saturday was one that hadn't even played before. Nic Cester from Aussie rock band Jet was assembling some mates to form what would soon be dubbed the 'Supergroup'. As well as Cester, the band included Kram from Spiderbait, Chris Cheney from The Living End, Davey Lane from You Am I and Pat Bourke from Dallas Crane. They would be performing something that was about as far removed from Missy's song as you could get: the Steve Wright classic 'Evie'. Our rollercoaster was coming together.

The concert's final line-up would be Noiseworks, Missy Higgins, Killing Heidi, Kasey Chambers (singing a spine-tingling version of Cyndi Lauper's 'True Colours'), the Supergroup, Guy Sebastian and Alex Lloyd. By any standard, that would make for one hell of a night. And just as well. Tickets had already sold out before we announced the final line-up and exactly 4500 people had each paid $25 to be there. We'd promised every cent would go straight to World Vision, meaning we'd already raised $112 500 before the telethon even started. And the audience watching from home was going to be much, much bigger than the one at the Opera House. The event would not only be seen on Australia's three commercial networks but, thanks to the ABC, in fifty-two countries around the world, including those hit hardest by the disaster.

Yoko and I took some time out to pinch ourselves—our little *Sunrise* project had turned into an unprecedented media event. At one point, Dave Masala wandered past and offered one of his classic understatements: 'Guess we'd better not fuck it up.' By the end of the week, 650 people were working behind the scenes and around the clock to make sure we didn't.

Two of those people were director Graeme Rowland and his assistant, Vanessa Field. For two entire days, they remained inside a small room at Martin Place, with recordings of each song to be performed on the night. They listened to them over and over again—each song probably a dozen times. Rowland would be in command of fifteen cameras around the Opera House stage. Some would be on cranes, so he could get big, sweeping shots across the crowd. Some would be up close to the performers and others would glide along tracks. He'd even have one in the sky, aboard the Channel Seven chopper. He wanted a solid plan to get the most from each camera. As he and Field listened to the songs, they took detailed notes on what shot would suit any particular moment—a process known as shot blocking. Rowland felt this would ensure the show went off without a hitch.

Then it was Friday, 7 January—the day before the broadcast. Cast and crew converged on the Opera

House for a full rehearsal. A similar dry run, for the telethon, was happening at Telstra Dome in Melbourne.

David Koch was looking worried, pacing around the hosting platform by the harbour. I thought perhaps he was nervous about broadcasting to such a large audience; it was certainly the biggest thing we'd ever done. Instead, he told me he was 'scared shitless' about hosting alongside industry stalwarts like Larry Emdur and Richard Wilkins—in early 2005, we still considered ourselves a rather humble little breakfast show. At times like these, an executive producer needs to come up with words of wisdom, so I just laughed and told him he was cute. I think it did the trick.

The rehearsal went remarkably well, apart from Guy Sebastian missing his spot because of traffic on the Harbour Bridge. That was no big deal; all of the performers would be spending the night at a hotel alongside the venue. As the day was wrapping up, I took a call from Vince Foti. He and his brother were the undisputed masters of lighting up the sky and, just a week earlier, they'd wowed the world by having the Sydney Harbour Bridge erupt for New Year's Eve. He was offering to donate a fireworks display. Naturally, we accepted. The concert may well have been the biggest thing my team had produced but, in many ways, it was also the easiest. People couldn't do enough to help; you could feel a real sense of community. It had become much more than a TV show.

The big day arrived and we had reason to be confident: the three television networks were working well together; the Sydney and Melbourne rehearsals had gone to plan; even the weather was looking good. Things seemed almost too perfect.

Two hours before the gates were due to open, we realised we didn't have anyone to collect tickets from the 4500 people lining up outside. Nobody on our team could be spared, as they all had assigned roles. Dave Masala took care of it in a way only he could have. He sent our head of security, Jim Fidler, to Bondi Beach. Fidler returned with fifteen backpackers, who we paid and fed to get everyone through the gate.

At 6.30pm, we went live across Australia and throughout Asia.

We opened with a fast-moving shot from the Channel Seven helicopter. Viewers could see the sun setting behind the Harbour Bridge and hear a hint of distant cheering. That cheering grew louder as the chopper kept moving. Within seconds, it was hovering above one of Australia's most famous icons. The cheering was about to reach its climax. We segued straight to centre stage, to one of the most well-known riffs in Australian rock. Thousands of arms were now in the air, hands clapping in unison to a classic Noiseworks hit. The band's front man, Jon Stevens, had lost none of his sex appeal. He worked the crowd like a god, before telling them to reach out and touch somebody.

'I've never seen energy like it,' remembers Graeme Rowland. 'Our two days of shot blocking went out the window because we just had to capture the atmosphere.' I was standing behind Rowland in the broadcast truck, and started jumping up and down. There's nothing like an excited executive producer to get in the way of people doing serious work.

Cameras were instructed to get wide shots of the crowd, and you could see the passion on people's faces. Glenn Pallister was watching from the master control room at Channel Nine. I could hear him in my headphones, repeatedly saying, 'Fuck, man, this is brilliant.' He wasn't the only one loving it. We'd only been on the air a few minutes before Leckie was on the phone. 'How great is this? It's fucking great.' I could hardly hear him over the noise.

When Stevens stopped singing, the crowd took over. They knew every word and sang them loudly. The Noiseworks singer stood there in awe, perhaps remembering his days on top. At the last beat of the drum, the cheering again erupted, as he issued one last instruction: 'Dig deep, Australia, and reach out!'

It was clear that David Koch was over his nerves. As the camera panned to our hosts, he was on his feet, cheering with everyone else. Kochie, Mel and Larry Emdur were on a platform about 100 metres from the main stage, so they could talk without being drowned out by the crowd. The same couldn't be said for Gretel Killeen. We crossed to her in the mosh pit but could hear only the hundreds of people swarming around her. There's no doubt all the noise would have been disturbing the more genteel performances underway inside the Opera House. Gretel threw to Richard Wilkins backstage. At least, we think she did. We simply switched away when her mouth stopped moving. Richard was with Jon Stevens, who still had sweat dripping from his brow. 'There's a lotta love at the Opera House,' Stevens told him. 'This kind of tragedy just cuts through the soul.'

From there, we handed over to Melbourne. I can't tell you much about what they did; in between each performance, we were scrambling to get the stage ready for the next. The time between each song seemed to fly, but still not quickly enough for David Leckie. As he watched some of Australia's biggest celebrities joke around at the telethon, he called to order they throw straight back to Sydney. He told me he was getting bored and missing the energy from the Opera House. He had a point but it wasn't that simple. First, we weren't ready to take back control, and even if we were, it wasn't our choice. Nine was in charge of the rundown. I tried explaining this but Leckie lost interest in the conversation.

Midway through the night, Eddie, Andrew and Rove crossed to Molly Meldrum in Phuket. Molly was with a group of Thai locals who'd lit candles down by the beach. They sat in a semicircle and looked out towards the ocean. Everything seemed so calm. It was hard to imagine the now-gentle waves could have risen with such intensity just a week earlier. It was a sombre, yet beautiful moment. But, as much as I love him, you can always count on things going wrong when Molly is involved. The Channel Nine producer had told him to keep on talking until he received a cue to stop. That would have worked fine but for the fact his earpiece had fallen out and he hadn't noticed. We were watching from the truck at the Opera House and could tell something was wrong. He kept talking and talking and talking. Even by Molly's standards, it was dragging on. You could see on his face that he was waiting to be told to stop, but did his best to follow his earlier instructions. Well after the cross was meant to be over, he gave up waiting. He just looked at the camera and, with his typical honesty, declared, 'Look, there's not much more I can say.' There was a sigh of relief in the control room.

As the night went on, the donations got bigger: the tally was no longer in the thousands, but in the millions, of dollars. Big business also stepped up, with companies like ANZ and NAB contributing $1 million each. ANZ's chief executive, John McFarlane, gave a personal donation of $250000. Just as touching were the kids handing over their piggybank savings and the couple who asked guests at their wedding to donate money to the appeal, rather than buy gifts.

The emotive power of the performances no doubt played a part in so much money being donated to the cause. Guy Sebastian had made the right choice of song; you could feel his passion. He later told viewers, 'It makes you think, man, life is so fragile. It makes you think about God and makes you think about your faith.' To me, the standout performance was from Missy Higgins. For the first time that night, the crowd fell silent as Missy sang from behind her piano.

> And we could only see each other, we'll breathe together,
>
> These arms will not be taught to need another's,
>
> 'Cause we're the special two.

Watching from outside the truck, I saw a man in the crowd wipe away a tear. Missy was just as moved. 'I've got goosebumps all over me,' she said afterwards.

The night ended with Alex Lloyd performing his hit song 'Amazing', modified to include the line 'Australia, you've been amazing'. As he reached the final chorus, Graeme Rowland gave the Foti brothers the signal. Fireworks started blasting above the Opera House at just the right moment. Alex looked up and smiled.

The screen faded to black with the words 'Thank you Australia'.

Almost nine million people had tuned into the event in Australia alone. When the phone lines closed, we'd raised $20 106 030.

World Vision's Tim Costello was elated, declaring that Australia had set the benchmark for tsunami aid. 'For perhaps the first time in our history, Australia is actually so far out in front, it's magnificent.' Television host Andrew Denton, who was part of the Melbourne telethon, summed it up: 'The really good thing about tonight is that just as the world seemed like it was losing its head, it's found its heart.'

I received calls from senior people at Nine and Ten, including Nine's CEO, David Gyngell, congratulating my team. There was nothing from Leckie; the last I heard from him had been when he was at home, getting bored. Still, without him the night would never have happened.

For many of us, that broadcast was the proudest of our careers—we'd used our positions to make a real difference to people's lives. When we finally wrapped later that night, some of us ended up at a bar not far from Circular Quay. I walked in to see Yael Cohn clinking glasses with my mum, who'd been part of the crowd. They'd clearly already shared a bottle or two, and were musing that we'd just witnessed a turning point in the way the media operates. 'Everyone working together for the greater good,' was how Yael put it.

It turned out to be false hope. By Monday morning, the love-in was over. It was back to cutthroat world of network television.

7

TAKE THE WEATHER WITH YOU

As a kid, I was always a fan of the Leyland brothers. Like millions of other Australians, I'd watch as Mike and Mal *travelled all over the countryside* in their orange Kombi. For many living in the city, the Channel Nine series provided a glimpse into parts of Australia they wouldn't otherwise see.

In late 2004, I drew inspiration from the Leylands, by sending Grant Denyer and producer Paula Crawford on a twelve-month odyssey. The idea was simple enough: jump in a campervan and head clockwise around the country. Every morning, Grant would present the weather from wherever they happened to be. I figured it would be a good way to connect with our viewers outside Sydney. As much as I liked our Martin Place studio, I worried it was a long way from middle Australia.

'I think you were nervous about pitching the idea to us,' remembers Paula. 'You kept saying, "You need to think very, very carefully about this because your lives will not be the same." Grant and I looked at each other and, in an instant, said, "Yes, we're doing it!"'

The *Sunrise* Weather Wagon, as it became known, set off from Sydney on Monday, 22 November 2004. It was hard to miss—Grant's smiling face was plastered across either side. A satellite truck followed the campervan wherever it went, which was the key to broadcasting from anywhere.

Apart from Grant and Paula, the team included a cameraman, sound recordist and a satellite operator. Paul Slater was one of the wagon's first cameramen. 'It sounds glamorous,' he says, 'but it was really hard work.' They were up each morning at four-thirty, before doing satellite checks with the Sydney control room from 5am. Grant's first live report each day was at 6am. He then did one every thirty minutes until 8.30am, before spending another thirty minutes signing autographs and posing for photos with locals. Plenty of them showed up each day, as Grant's fame continued to rise.

After the show, the team hit the road for drives that sometimes went on for six hours (each crew member took turns driving—even Grant). They then spent three hours shooting and editing vision of their destination, to be used the following morning. But, as Paul reveals, 'Somehow, we'd still go out and have twenty beers and operate on just two hours' sleep.' Paula says that what happens on tour stays on tour but concedes,

'We had a few nights in pubs that we probably shouldn't have had.'

You could never tell on air. Grant's star shone every day; no matter how small the town or how big the city, he found ways of making us laugh. But while everything he did on television seemed spontaneous, he'd usually planned every second. As Paula puts it, 'You see the light go on in his eyes and know mischief is about to happen.' But, sometimes, even Grant didn't know what was coming. During a visit to a salmon farm in Tasmania, he intended to take a leaf out of sporting legend Rex Hunt's book by giving a fish a kiss before tossing it back in the water. But when Grant threw it back, the fish started floating. His kiss had somehow killed it. The salmon farmer laughed—he'd never seen anything like it.

Over the years, Grant got used to people comparing him to Lleyton Hewitt, as they had a similar build and features. So, as the weather wagon passed through Melbourne during the Australian Open, Paul Slater thought they should take things to the next level. They got a mullet wig from Seven's makeup department, then raided the local Nike store for one of Lleyton's trademark shirts and caps. The impersonation was uncanny; Grant nailed not just Lleyton's look but his mannerisms and attitude. It was good enough to trick many people at Melbourne Park, including local socialite Lillian Frank, who congratulated him on an overnight win. Even Andy Roddick did a double take while warming up on an outside court, and Grant yelled out to him—'You're going down, Roddick.'

The practical jokes weren't limited to the ones on air. During their long drives, someone would inevitably fall asleep. When they later woke, it could be with a wet patch on their pants. Dripping water onto someone's crotch became a rite of passage for anyone new on the crew. More seriously, though, the antics were a distraction from not just their seemingly never-ending journey but from their simmering frustrations with colleagues in Sydney. They often felt the rest of the *Sunrise* team didn't appreciate the effort that went into life on the road.

If interviews that Kochie and Mel were conducting went longer than their allocated time, Grant would be the one to suffer. The duration of his crosses were sometimes slashed in half, with just thirty seconds' notice. That was despite the fact that he may have planned for live interviews of his own or for stunts that required more than his shortened allocation. It particularly upset the weather team when Sydney decided not to run stories that they'd sacrificed sleep to edit. Paul Slater says, 'If you spend hours working on something only to see it dropped at the last second, of course it's going to be annoying.' To be fair to the control room producers in Sydney, it was their job to take a big-picture view, and the weather team had no way of knowing what was happening more broadly in the show.

There were times when line producer David 'Dougie' Walters slashed more than just a minute or two. Former *Sunrise* staffer Alicia Malone (now a Hollywood-based showbiz correspondent) once invited Grant to report from her pole-dancing class. During his first cross for the morning, Grant assured our viewers that it was a legitimate sport used by many to get fit, but the dance hall's red lights probably didn't help his case. Back in the studio, Mel was particularly uncomfortable. The normal on-air banter with Grant was missing, and she quickly moved on to the next segment with barely a smile. During a commercial break, she complained to Dougie that watching girls in skimpy clothes slide up and down poles didn't pass what we called the 'Coco Pops test'—in other words, content suitable for families. Rather than persevere with awkward television, Dougie dropped Grant for the rest of the morning. Mel and Kochie read the remaining weather reports back in the studio, without explaining why. Many viewers probably guessed, though.

It was rare for Dougie to shorten crosses that were pulling at heartstrings, however. In September 2005, Grant broadcast live from Wyndham, which is the northernmost town of the Kimberley region and about 2000 kilometres from Perth. The local school was preparing to launch a radio station when the *Sunrise* weather team passed through. The teachers hoped the station would help boost their students' confidence and language skills, as the kids, many of them

Indigenous, were often reluctant to share their feelings. Grant's final live report that morning was from alongside the weather wagon. About fifty kids counted down from ten, and he then switched on the wagon's radio, to hear the first sounds from the school radio station. One of the teachers shed a tear just out of camera range. He later said it was overwhelming to see the rest of the country acknowledging the kids. 'We went out and touched real people's lives and we brought those lives to people across Australia,' says Paula Crawford. 'We found these amazing stories that other people weren't telling. That's why it was so special.'

After Wyndham, the plan was for the wagon to be transported to Darwin. Grant, Paula and the rest of the team would spend some time with their families in Sydney while it was moved across. But, first, they had to get back to Perth aboard a small six-seater plane. Before taking off, the two pilots warned them they were in for a bumpy ride; a fierce storm was moving through the area. The *Sunrise* team scoffed that wouldn't faze them—they covered weather for a living. Midway through the flight, Paula noticed one of the pilots reaching for a folder of paper charts. 'I remember thinking, *That's strange. Why does he need paper charts?* They kept looking at each other without saying anything to us,' she says.

The storm had knocked out many of the plane's navigation systems. They made it to Perth but then had a new problem: the pilots weren't sure whether their wheels were down, as the indicator lights had stopped working. They declared it was an emergency. 'When the pilot told us to practise our brace position, we all thought it was a joke,' says Paula. 'Grant asked me whether I had any last wishes.' They realised it wasn't a joke when they saw fire trucks and ambulances lining the runway below. The control tower could see that the landing gear was down but nobody knew whether the wheels had actually locked in position. Everyone on the weather team held on to their ankles as the plane touched down, safely.

Almost a year to the day after it left, the weather wagon arrived back in Sydney. The team had successfully circled the country; along the way, they showcased more than 200 towns and interviewed more than 2500 people. 'It was the best job of my life,' Paula says. 'The characters and the country. I loved every second.'

***

The weather wagon's retirement didn't mean Grant's job was done.

On Saturday, 18 March 2006, we were keeping a close eye on a cyclone that was nudging closer to Queensland's far north. We knew Cyclone Larry was going to be big but had no way of knowing where on the coast it would cross. With only hours before the region's airports were to be closed, we sent Grant and a small team to Townsville. We wanted them in position, in case the cyclone hit before Monday's show. Once that happened, there'd be no way in or out for days.

The punt paid off.

Cyclone Larry crossed the coast near Innisfail while *Sunrise* was going to air on Monday. We were in Melbourne that morning for a special show from the Commonwealth Games. It was meant to feature interviews with sporting stars and a live performance from Pink. But, as reports emerged of widespread damage, we ditched everything in our rundown.

Grant Denyer was the only television reporter able to broadcast live from the worst-affected area, as our competitors had left it too late to get people and equipment in. Viewers watched as he got soaked by torrential rain, which, at times, was so fierce that the satellite signal broke up. Producers also scrambled to line up phone interview after phone interview with anyone in the region. They called pubs, homes, service stations—anybody who picked up went straight on the air. Many gave harrowing accounts of hearing or watching their homes being ripped apart.

Pink was sitting on the studio floor, watching it unfold. 'I kept being asked to go and apologise to her,' says Paula. 'Three times I went over and three times she said, "Listen, people's lives are being affected. That is far more important than me performing." I've been a big fan of hers ever since.'

Over on Nine, *Today* chose to stick with its coverage of the Commonwealth Games. The studio-based weather presenter reported that Far North Queensland was likely to get some strong winds and heavy rain. That was putting it lightly—it was one of the worst natural disasters in decades. *Today'* s viewers only had to switch to *Sunrise* to see it for themselves—and most did. Our commercial-free coverage continued well beyond 9am and long after *Today* had gone off air.

I wasn't going to give them any chance to play catch-up.

The following morning, we interviewed a State Emergency Service commander in Innisfail, who revealed the biggest problem they had was a shortage of manpower. *Sunrise* then did what only *Sunrise* could.

I placed a call to Qantas and asked them to give us a plane. We wanted to fill it with skilled tradies from around Australia for a mercy dash to Far North Queensland. The airline said yes—and so did the tradies. Thousands of them. *Sunrise* producers spent a week assembling the right mix of electricians, carpenters, engineers and plumbers. We also had to work with authorities in the affected area to make sure the *Sunrise* tradies had assigned roles. Insurance issues proved to be the biggest hurdle. In the end, the Queensland government promised to cover the risk.

Kochie broadcast live from the Qantas hangar at Brisbane Airport on 27 March. The plane wasn't just loaded with people but with things like generators and tools. We'd been inundated with donations. A labourer from Bribie Island told Kochie that his local mower shop had loaned him a chainsaw for the trip. And Qantas wasn't the only big company to lend a hand. Our hotel partner, Accor, offered free accommodation to everyone on the plane, and accommodation in itself was a logistical challenge. The tradies were spread across six hotels, with *Sunrise* -rented buses shuttling between each. The volunteer workers spent a week in the region. They removed fallen trees, rebuilt fences, fixed roofs and, above all, helped bring some sense of optimism to people who had been through so much.

General Peter Cosgrove, who was co-ordinating the broader relief effort, told our reporter, Monique Wright, that Operation *Sunrise* 'showed that working Australians have a heart as big as the outdoors.' A few months later, he joined David Koch for a return visit to the region. They were guests of honour at a local fundraiser at the Innisfail Town Hall and were invited on stage for what was supposedly a Far North Queensland tradition: Kochie and the man who would go on to be our governor-general took part in a five-minute chicken dance. The locals thought it was a scream.

Just as with *Australia Unites:Reach Out to Asia,* *Sunrise* had served as a catalyst. People wanted to help; we simply gave them a way to do it.

8

UP A RIDGE, THEN DOWN A RIDGE

The fact that people doubted two rival frontbenchers could be friends said much about Australian politics. We were often asked, as their rapport grew during their weekly *Sunrise* segments, whether Kevin Rudd and Joe Hockey were really mates. But there was one place their mateship was proved beyond question: the Kokoda Track.

Linking the north and south coasts of Papua New Guinea, the bush trail served as the ultimate test of the courage and endurance of Australian soldiers during the Second World War. For four long months, the Australians held off a determined and better-resourced Japanese force trying to reach Port Moresby. It was a bloody and desperate conflict waged in the most difficult of conditions. The track was little more than a single dirt path through thick rainforest, winding its way for 96 kilometres across the Owen Stanley Range.

Young Australian soldier Barney Findlay wrote a letter home on 9 November 1942, in which he tried to describe the painful trek:

We go up a ridge then down a ridge and up a ridge again. It was the cruellest day I have ever spent in my life. Each time I stopped, my calves cramped and by the time I had walked the cramp away, I'd get a cramp again. You might ask why I or anyone else kept going. You kept going because you have to.

More than 600 Australians lost their lives along the Kokoda Track, some while trying to pull injured mates to safety. At least a thousand were seriously hurt.

David Koch, a passionate student of Australia's wartime history, had long wanted to trek it himself. And, in 2006, he challenged Kevin Rudd and Joe Hockey to join him. They'd spend six days walking towards the Isurava Memorial, where they'd arrive in time for an Anzac Day service. All of it would be filmed for *Sunrise.*

The three of them trained for three months—sometimes together, but usually on their own. They went on bushwalks, and ran up and down steps with backpacks loaded with weights. My best friend and flatmate, Steven Claus, would be one of the cameramen, so he too was torturing his body. I'd arrive home at night to see him emerge from our high-rise building's fire stairs, covered in sweat.

They were part of a bigger expedition group—about twenty in all—that gathered at Brisbane Airport on Tuesday, 18 April for the trip to Papua New Guinea.

For Rudd and Kochie, it would be a family affair. The shadow foreign minister brought his nineteen-year-old son, Nicholas, while Kochie was travelling with his son AJ, brother Matt and nephew Harry.

The flight took about three hours. Most on board listened to music or flicked through magazines, but not Kevin Rudd. He spent the entire time reading the Bible. Perhaps he'd heard the weather report and was seeking help from above; the tail of a cyclone was still dumping huge amounts of rain along the track. Walking it was tough at the best of times, but now they'd face the added burden of mud. They got a taste before even taking a step. A small bus tried to get them as close as possible to the start of the track, but kept getting bogged.

Most expeditions start on the north coast and work their way south, because of the number of small villages in the north. They are good places to take time out while everyone gets used to the conditions. The *Sunrise* team, though, would be starting from the southern end, near Port Moresby, in order to reach Isurava on Anzac Day. There's nothing friendly about the south, which is considered too dense to live in. For the first couple of days, the trekkers would see few signs of habitation.

At the start, the group was in high spirits. They took a few photos and prepped to start walking. Everyone was dressed in black shirts (provided by the expedition company) and all wore the same type of cap. All, that is, except Joe Hockey. He was wearing an Aussie bush hat that was big enough to tape a photo in its pouch, of his baby son, Xavier. His fellow trekkers jibed that he was nothing but a big softie. Just thirty minutes into the trek, their smiles were gone. Hockey was breathless as he looked up at Steven's camera to declare, 'This is bloody hard work.'

And it was made harder by the mud. Midway through the morning, they encountered a lowland swamp that took hours to pass. The mud was like a vacuum, making every step an effort. For some, it almost reached their knees. Hill slopes were no less difficult. It was often hard to get traction because the ground just kept slipping. Kochie fell five times and broke both his hiking sticks.

Those with the toughest jobs were Steven and his fellow cameraman, David Thompson. The pair had reunited after working together at Channel Ten in Cairns in the late 1990s. David had been a frequent visitor to Papua New Guinea, including with me, to cover the 1998 tsunami, but this was his first time walking the track. The trek leader, Brian Freeman, was ex-military, and wanted to maintain a steady and disciplined pace. That made life difficult for Steven and David, who were trying to shoot enough material for *Sunrise.* 'We had to keep leapfrogging everyone,' recalls David. 'That's really hard to do. Not only is the track single-file but we were still struggling just to walk the thing ourselves.' They ended up working through breaks, including lunch, to get enough shots. 'It was just unbelievably miserable.'

It was miserable, too, for Queenslander Ian Thomason. He was walking just ahead of Kevin Rudd late on the first day when he was struck by a falling branch. His calf muscle soon became, what Rudd described as, 'the size of a pawpaw'. Thomason was given the option of heading back but vowed to push on. That, he said, was the point of Kokoda.

As the team reached base camp, they were soaked and exhausted. Rudd was heard to say, 'Punishing, really punishing,' before he stumbled onto his knee. Joe Hockey was faring no better. His face was red and his body in pain. 'Physically,' he said, 'that was the toughest day of my life.'

Dinner that night didn't bring much relief. As bowls were passed around, they quickly filled with rainwater. The food was mush but had to be eaten. One trekker described having to make themselves eat as like feeding a baby that really doesn't want to be fed. You just fill your mouth and force yourself to swallow. The tents were small and pitched in mud. Everyone tried to remove their revolting mud-stained clothes before rushing inside, but they were never quick enough to keep the rain out.

Complaining was pointless. And, besides, what they were going through gave everyone a better insight into the struggles faced by our soldiers in 1942. Joe Hockey said as much when he reflected on the day for *Sunrise:* 'For me, there was a spiritual moment as the rain was coming into the valley. You couldn't help but think of the last gasp defence by the Australians as literally thousands of Japanese walked into the valley with lanterns and encircled them. Absolute heroics.'

The second day was no less difficult. Rivers and creeks were swollen after a fortnight of heavy rain. That made them tricky to cross. One in particular looked like it would be near impossible. The group was travelling with 'porters', who'd come down from a village in the country's north. Resourceful by nature, they offered a solution: a makeshift bridge created out of vines and branches. One by one, the trekkers made their way across, each holding hands with the locals. That wasn't enough to steady one walker, who plunged into the rushing water below. Four porters jumped in after him and pulled him to safety. Joe Hockey watched all this unfold and had serious fears about using the bridge. He sat on the river's edge for a good five minutes before accepting he had little choice. There were porters either side of him and others lining the bank as he carefully considered each step. He only started breathing again when he reached the other side.

As the expedition continued, a second *Sunrise* team was having problems of its own. We intended to make history on Anzac Day by becoming the first show to broadcast live from the Kokoda Track. Many, including some of our colleagues at Seven, said it couldn't be done.

Producer Paula Crawford was determined to prove them wrong. She was in Port Moresby with our satellite equipment and generators. Her plan was to reach Isurava ahead of the expedition, to set up for our special outside broadcast. The only way that could be done was with a heavy-duty helicopter capable of lifting an immense amount of weight. The day before Paula's team was due to depart, word came through that the same type of chopper had crashed in the same type of area that they were heading. The pilot was trying to fly out of a valley when his view was blocked by fast-moving cloud. Three people were killed and four others injured. The chopper belonged to the same company that we were using. 'That meant they were being very, very cautious in taking us in,' Paula says. 'The weather kept us grounded for two days and we were worried that time was running out. Thankfully, there was finally a break in the cloud and we were able to reach Isurava.'

That break in the weather meant the trekkers were no longer battling teeming rain. Sadly, it came too late to avoid something far more troubling. Almost everyone developed something that resembled frostbite. Constant dampness and friction had peeled back their outer layer of skin, removing protection from bacteria. 'It was disgusting,' says Steven Claus. 'Our feet had red blotches all over them. It was really painful, like you had a stack of razorblades stuck in your boot.'

Kochie was hit particularly hard. His feet became so swollen that he could no longer tie up his shoes, and could do little more than wrap the laces around his ankles. A Sydney medic accompanied the expedition but he'd only brought a single tube of Hydrozole, which did nothing to ease everyone's pain. Some sought relief at the end of each day by jumping into streams for bush baths. One afternoon, Kevin Rudd lost his footing and was sucked downstream by the current. Joe Hockey reached out to grab him, before yelling, 'I've got money from Beazley to let you go!' Kim Beazley was opposition leader at the time and most expected Rudd would soon challenge him for the job.

David Koch, on the other hand, was struggling to form a bond with Rudd's son, Nicholas. The two were walking close together one morning when Kochie tried to strike up a conversation. In his typical blokey way, he first asked Nick about his favourite footy team. He didn't have one. 'What about movies?' asked Kochie, but got no further. Running out of options, he asked Nick what *did* interest him. 'Collecting antique jewellery,' was the unexpected response. Kochie thought to himself, *Fuck, I have nowhere to go with that.* He soon got over this when he discovered Nick possessed a far more useful quality than being able to talk about football: optimism. On days when many felt down, it was Nick who brought them back up with words of support. Hockey told Rudd that if his new son, Xavier, grew up to be anything like Nicholas, he'd be a happy man. Nick was later voted the group's most popular trekker.

As the group reached the country's north, they started to encounter local villages. They weren't large, by any means: most consisted of just a few pole houses and some chooks scratching around below. But one afternoon, David Thompson was walking ahead when he heard what he describes as 'beautiful, beautiful singing filtering through the forest'. He followed his ears to a small village church. The pastor spotted him and invited him inside. 'I was so embarrassed telling them I can't come in because I'm filthy and I stink,' David remembers. 'But the pastor kept saying, "We don't care, please come in."'

And, luckily, he did. Sitting in the front row of the congregation was a frail man in his nineties who was doing his best to sing along. His name was Mr Oridiki and he was one of the few remaining Fuzzy Wuzzy Angels. Aussie diggers gave the Koiari people that nickname because of their frizzy hair and repeated acts of valiance during the war. Without the Fuzzy Wuzzies, the Australian death toll would have been even higher. They risked their own lives not only to deliver supplies but to carry wounded soldiers to safety. David introduced his new friend to his fellow trekkers when they reached the village. Joe Hockey shook Mr Oridiki's hand, while repeatedly saying, 'Thank you, thank you.'

That night, everyone was sitting around a campfire, sharing personal stories. Some talked about family, others about their jobs. When they got to Rudd, he started singing.

> Oh, Danny Boy, the pipes, the pipes are calling
> From glen to glen and down the mountain side,
> The summer's gone, and all the roses falling,
> It's you, it's you must go and I must bide.

Those who were there say he clearly sang from the heart. Rudd felt 'Danny Boy' was fitting after their earlier encounter at the village.

Paula Crawford was busy at Isurava, preparing for the live broadcast, now just two days away. 'The place has such a sense of history without you even knowing the stories,' she says. 'It's profoundly moving.' The memorial itself must be one of the most beautiful in the world. It sits above a vast valley and is perfectly centred within a gap of the mountain range. Its impact is strengthened by the simplicity of its design—just four black granite pillars. Each is inscribed with single word: Courage, Endurance, Mateship and Sacrifice.

Paula and her team weren't the only ones who were already at Isurava. Others making the journey had set up camp after walking from the track's northern starting point. That night, they all gathered around a big white sheet that doubled as a projection screen. They watched old footage from the Kokoda campaign shot not far from where they now sat. 'All of a sudden, I had a feeling of people behind me,' says Paula. 'I turned around to see some local villagers. And they were all murmuring about something in the vision.' They'd recognised some of their relatives. Paula was amazed: 'They were pointing out their grandfathers and great-grandfathers. People who'd helped the Australians during the war.'

Back on the track, the major talking point remained the mud. 'We started labelling different types of mud after curries,' says Steven Claus. 'There was butter chicken mud, Mongolian lamb mud and korma mud. I think it also goes to show how much we were craving real food.'

Kevin Rudd was craving real sleep. As the sun rose on 24 April, a local rooster stumbled across the camp and was only too happy to serve as an alarm clock. Rudd was having none of it. His screaming could be heard bouncing off the hills: 'Someone fucking shut that fucking rooster up or I will fucking shoot it!'

David Koch yelled back, 'Morning, Kevin!'

Later that day, they came across something they'll never forget. It was a small plaque that read: 'Lt Thomas Harold (Butch) Bisset. 10th Platoon, B Company, 2/14 AIF. Died of wounds suffered during the Battle for Isurava in the arms of his brother, Captain Stan Bisset, on August 30, 1942.'

Butch and Stan had fought in the Middle East, before being deployed together to Papua New Guinea. Butch was a platoon commander and Stan an intelligence officer. Both had control of groups of men within the same battalion. They'd been given the job of relieving Australian soldiers who'd been fending off the Japanese at Isurava for weeks. The first challenge was simply to reach them. Stan later said:

> We had some stiff climbs in some of the rugged mountains in Syria, but this was much worse. The weather and the thick mud were appalling. The men perspired so much they were completely dehydrated at the end of the day and had to be issued with salt tablets on a daily basis.

The battalion reached Isurava on 27 August 1942 and was confronted by what Stan called 'fierce waves' of Japanese fighters. 'We were expecting about 1500 Japanese but by the time we got to Isurava, their strength had grown to about 8000. We were vastly outnumbered.'

In the space of two days, they had to endure eleven separate Japanese attacks but somehow managed to hold their ground. Late on 29 August, Butch was handing out ammunition to his men when he came under fire from a Japanese machine gun. He was badly wounded. As others tried to pull him to safety, he ordered them away. Butch Bisset didn't want his men to be hit as well. They ignored him and managed to stretcher him to an area just off the main track.

Stan was only about 30 metres back but had no idea his brother was dying. He was busy trying to help another man, who'd lost a hand when a grenade went off prematurely. Word finally reached him that Butch was in trouble. He arrived to find him drifting in and out of consciousness, and stayed with his brother for six hours. 'We talked about Mum and Dad, our good times and bad times and what we did as kids,' Stan was later quoted as saying. 'I sat with him until about 4am when he finally left us. We buried him beside the track.'

David Koch stood silently in front of the plaque, to reflect on the sacrifices made by the brothers. 'The trek was bad enough for us,' he said later. 'Imagine doing it late at night while under heavy fire. Those guys were heroes and they did it for us.'

The *Sunrise* expedition group walked into Isurava on the eve of Anzac Day. David Thompson was the first one out. 'There were all these people looking at me. I felt like a primal animal coming out of the forest.' Paula Crawford saw him and ran to give him a hug. 'I was really worried about my disgusting, mud-covered condition,' David says, 'so I tried to repel her. But it was no use, she was too excited to care.' The rest of the team weren't far behind him. They'd endured six days of physical and, at times, emotional pain to get there. Paula remembers some of the trekkers wiping away tears.

That night, the rain returned. And in a big way. Our satellite technicians warned that if it didn't stop by morning, they wouldn't get a signal. The live broadcast wouldn't happen. As the exhausted trekkers fell into a deep sleep, Paula was awake in her tent, writing the final order of the Anzac service. She jokes about how there were no photocopiers in Isurava, so she had to write it five times over, using nothing more than the light of a torch. David Thompson and Steven Claus were woken at 4am, to set up for the broadcast. As they emerged from their tents, there wasn't a cloud in the sky.

Back in Sydney, I saw their first pictures just after 5am and remember thinking this kind of thing was why I loved my job. *Sunrise* was about to make history. It hadn't come cheap and that was money we'd never get back, after refusing to seek sponsors for such a sacred event. We even dropped our usual commercial breaks. It had been a big risk, given there were no guarantees our plan would work.

At 6am, David Koch welcomed our audience to Isurava. When he first appeared, many in the office were taken aback by how drained he looked. We also thought he'd lost weight. Kevin Rudd and Joe Hockey were just as dishevelled. It was quite a contrast to how we're used to seeing politicians.

Broadcasting the service was anything but conventional. We didn't have a floor manager and the Isurava team had limited communications with the

Sydney control room. They were pretty much on their own. It was up to Steven, David, Paula and sound recordist James Petch to make things work. We'd simply broadcast whatever they sent. Even though Paula had written out the order of service, it was too hard for Steven and David to read while shooting. She ended up talking them through the service, using a walkie-talkie and headphones. She'd tell them who to shoot and when. 'I tried my best to whisper,' she says, 'but I still got a few dirty looks.'

We televised the entire service. Former chaplain of the Australian Army Monsignor John Butler paid tribute to those who'd served, by talking about mateship. 'They may not have invented the word,' he mused, 'but they certainly showed us how to live it. Mateship takes the word friendship and elevates it to a higher plane.' Joe Hockey, clearly touched by his encounter with Mr Oridiki, read a poem by Sapper Bert Beros: 'May the mothers of Australia when they offer up a prayer mention those impromptu angels with the fuzzy wuzzy hair.'

Peter Meakin and I watched from his office. We both felt it was beautiful television. But, as the morning went on, we started to get emails from viewers who weren't as impressed. In fact, many accused us of showing a lack of respect. Some complained that Kochie, Kevin and Joe should have shaved, but far more were outraged by what they were wearing. Our expedition company had instructed the trekkers to leave their clothing in Port Moresby. Everyone was then handed a black shirt emblazoned with both the company's and Channel Seven's logo (which they'd pinched from our website). The guides insisted that wearing the 'uniform' was important, in case anything went wrong. With various groups on the track at the same time, the shirts enabled porters or medics to instantly identify who was who, and other groups on the track that week were wearing uniforms of their own. Emailers accused us of 'cashing in' on Anzac Day, by blatantly showing logos during a Dawn Service. One said it was commercialism at its grossest and 'a desecration of Australia's remembrance of those who served and died'.

I can guarantee you that commercialism was the last thing on our minds.

Midway through the show, Kochie tried to explain things on air and couldn't help conveying his disappointment:

> Anyway, in hindsight, we should've flown in a change of clothes with our satellite equipment for the service itself. It was obviously never our intention to take away from the significance of the day. Having just finished what we all considered a pilgrimage, the nature of Kokoda is understood and appreciated fully by all of us. The criticism comes as a big blow. I hope you accept my word that our intentions were genuine.

Many didn't.

The ABC's *Media Watch* program was among those to stick the boot in. Host Monica Attard dismissed our efforts: 'Courage, endurance, mateship and sacrifice. It would have been nice to see those four words on the shirts instead of an ad.'

Kochie, Hockey, Rudd and the rest of the group were despondent about the criticisms, but still proud of their achievement and humbled by the experience. It was an even more remarkable achievement for Ian Thomason, who'd injured his leg on day one. He finally got around to seeking proper medical help back in Brisbane, where doctors discovered he'd also fractured a rib.

When David Koch arrived home, a letter was waiting. It was from Stan Bisset. He wrote: 'I greatly appreciated viewing the excellent coverage of your rain soaked trek and the emotional service at Isurava. On behalf of the 2/14 Battalion Association, I would like to convey my congratulations to you on this very moving occasion. Thank you.'

With all the criticism over shirts, and the cynicism of our critics, Stan Bisset's view was the only one that mattered. To this day, that letter has pride of place in Kochie's Sydney office.

9

CITIZENS OF BEACONSFIELD

Tasmania is Australian television's blind spot, mainly because the commercial networks don't have any local stations there. Producers in Sydney who prepare national news bulletins can readily access stories from most other cities—but not from Hobart. They rely on the smaller Tasmanian stations to alert them to anything significant. In practice, producers on both sides of Bass Strait consider that more of a hassle than part of their routine. Still, there are a handful of Tasmanian stories that spike major mainland interest each year. In late April 2006, two such stories were happening at once.

The Targa Tasmania car rally is big business, with drivers from around the world heading south to disturb the peace. It's fast and furious, and not every car will finish. Spin-outs and crashes rate highly on sports channels, so cameras capture every moment. As sports reporters inhaled the fumes, a different media pack was preparing to cover a more sombre event—an anniversary of the worst kind. Ten years had passed since Australia's most infamous crime, the Port Arthur massacre. Survivors of Martin Bryant's rampage would be attending a televised ceremony on 28 April, so journalists flew in early to record interviews.

When news filtered through of a mine collapse in the state's north on 26 April, some of the travelling reporters thought it worth at least checking out. Most of them had never heard of Beaconsfield. Within a week, it would become the most talked-about town in Australia.

A thirty-minute drive from Launceston, Beaconsfield is home to just a few thousand people. Despite being at the heart of Tamar Valley, it's the sort of place you pass through on the way to somewhere else. It wasn't always like that, however. In the late nineteenth century, it was Tasmania's third-biggest town, thanks to the rush for gold. Miners were making a fortune and so was Beaconsfield. Dance halls and pubs did a roaring trade, as more and more families moved in. The town's luck ran out in 1914, not because of war but because of water. The deeper the miners dug, the more groundwater would flow. Their pumps proved useless and the shaft soon flooded. Too expensive to drain, the mine was abandoned and so was much of the town. It would take another eighty-four years for prospectors to return. The mine reopened in 1998. Things were hardly at the level of Beaconsfield's heyday, but 150 people did find work.

Come 2006, Beaconsfield was facing yet another change of fortune. Word around town was the mine could again shut; lower production and higher costs were taking a toll. For now, though, workers had a more immediate fear—constant underground drilling had triggered a time bomb. Rock falls were becoming more common, tunnels were collapsing and the ground seemed fragile.

Phil Malkin had worked in the mine since it reopened. He was good at his job and getting increasing responsibility. On 21 April 2006, he was acting shift leader, working at the deepest point of the mine. He'd been there before—plenty of times—but now something worried him. He could hear strange noises—a continuous rumble, echoing around the shaft. Malkin would later tell an inquest that the area 'made the hairs on the back of my neck stand up'. There's an old saying in mining: when you hear the earth talking, you don't talk back. You just get out of there. And that's exactly what Malkin did.

Four days later, the streets of Beaconsfield were lined with people from throughout the Tamar Valley for the Anzac Day parade. If you weren't watching it, you were probably in it. Locals reckon it gets bigger every year. Tradition is important to the people of Beaconsfield. Believers in solidarity, they honour the past in the hope their future will be strong. The town itself encircles the gold mine and, in particular, a large triangle of steel, known as a poppet head. The structure holds a giant wheel that cables people in and out of the shaft below.

At six o'clock that night, seventeen men lined up to head underground, ready to spend twelve hours in the world below. It's hard and dangerous work, but they knew the risks. They always shared a laugh on the way down while comparing their 'crib' (miner slang for food). They never came up for meal breaks.

For three of the men that night, the final stop would be 925 metres beneath the surface; that's three times the length of Sydney's Centrepoint Tower. Larry Knight, Todd Russell and Brant Webb were to spend the night netting the eastern side of a rock face. To do that, they'd need a specialised vehicle called a telehandler, which resembles a cherry picker. Larry was operating the vehicle, while Todd and Brant were in a basket at the front. At 9.20pm, Larry stepped off the telehandler, to load more mesh. Three minutes later, he was dead.

A small earthquake, later found to be the result of over-mining, caused the rock face to crumble. The forty-four-year-old father of three stood no chance against an avalanche of rubble. Todd and Brant would also have been crushed had it not been for the basket. It served as a precarious barrier to the rocks above.

The first media report of the collapse was in the *Launceston Examiner* on 26 April. Later that morning, a handful of Launceston journalists turned up for a small press conference. Mine manager Matthew Gill told them that three of his men were missing. Mike

Lester was a public relations consultant for the Beaconsfield mine. He would later write: 'Normally that is about as much media as you would expect in Tasmania. It was a terrible tragedy, but there have been other, bigger, mining disasters in Australia, including Tasmania.'

With so many mainland reporters visiting the state that week, though, it was inevitable the collapse would garner wider coverage. They arrived in Beaconsfield just after lunch. Most filed stories, but the mine collapse still wasn't headlining the 6pm news. Two days later, search crews found the body of Larry Knight. It now appeared likely that his two fellow miners were also dead. Again, the story was filed, but was still not the national lead.

Then, at 5.45pm on Sunday, 30 April, search crews heard a voice. It was Todd Russell: 'It's fucking cold and cramped in here! Get us out!'

The media was told at 7.30pm and, from that moment on, the so-called miracle at Beaconsfield became the only thing worth reporting. Authorities thought it would take around forty-eight hours for Todd and Brant, still beyond the reach of rescue crews, to be freed. This now had all the ingredients of a top story. The men were alive but still trapped and there was no foolproof plan to get them out. That kind of suspense makes for great television. Channel Seven had a news reporter at Beaconsfield, but I felt he wouldn't be enough. The Monday edition of *Sunrise* would be the next major program on air and I wanted to own the story.

I called Melissa Doyle, in the hope I could get her to Beaconsfield for Monday's show. David Koch had only just returned from Kokoda and needed time to recover. Melissa took the call while at home making dinner. I told her to pack an overnight bag and stand by the phone.

We still had a major hurdle. It was Sunday night and the last commercial flight from Sydney had already touched down in Tasmania. I paced with frustration before it hit me—if we couldn't get to Beaconsfield, then neither could our rival, *Today.* And that meant only one thing: we *had* to get to Beaconsfield.

Producing a breakfast television show is like playing a game of chess. You're constantly thinking of ways to outmanoeuvre your opponent. Default positions are useless; you need to work hard to win the loyalty of viewers. I asked a producer to find a plane we could charter that night. The jet took off from Sydney's Bankstown Airport with just one passenger: Melissa Doyle. Indulgent? Yes. Worth it? Without a doubt. Networks will sometimes fork out up to $100000 covering a major story. Knockout chess moves aren't cheap. It was a midnight shuttle, without the hindrance of curfews at either Bankstown or Launceston Airports. And, at 6am on Monday, the effort paid off.

As Australians switched on *Sunrise,* they saw their favourite breakfast host reporting from Beaconsfield. Not that there was much to report. There was no detail on the miners' condition, no information on how they'd get out and no comment from their families. The lone Channel Seven reporter could have handled the job, without the need for a high-profile presenter, but that wasn't the point. Melissa's presence in Beaconsfield helped create a perception that *Sunrise* was now the best source of information. Soon, that perception would also be the reality.

Within hours of us wrapping up that morning's show, the media circus roared into town. Journalists and camera crews were converging on Beaconsfield from every direction, most via that morning's commercial flights.

Seven News reporter Peter Morris is the man you want at every fast-moving story. He's better known as 'Zoomer'—a name he got while working at Channel Ten in the early 1990s. His cameramen found it hard to keep up as he zoomed from one story to the next. Zoomer doesn't do things by halves. His trip to Beaconsfield rivalled Melissa's. He'd lifted off from Melbourne at first light, aboard the Channel Seven helicopter. 'The flight was a feat on its own,' says Zoomer. 'It took us three or four hours. The pilot was worried about such a long flight, so we were hopping between King Island and various oil platforms in case something went wrong.' The chopper finally landed in a footy oval, right in the middle of Beaconsfield.

The media invasion was hard for such a small town to deal with. Mike Lester recalls: 'Rescue workers had to run the gauntlet past crowds of media cars, vans, journalists, photographers and television crews. Helicopters hovering above made it difficult to think and hear. People trying to get a few hours' sleep were sometimes woken by journalists banging on their doors, seeking interviews.'

The media can be a hungry beast. The less you feed it, the more it hunts. News editors back in Sydney and Melbourne were demanding better stories, and, with little new information, reporters would hound anyone in sight. 'Initially, the locals were very, very cagey,' says Zoomer. 'As a reporter, you go into a little town like Beaconsfield and they become a closed shop, a closed community.'

By Monday afternoon, it was becoming obvious that Todd and Brant would be trapped for more than forty-eight hours. Layers of thick rock stood between the pair and their rescuers. Engineers were trying to work out how to get through the rock without causing a further collapse. Our viewers were captivated and had so many questions. What were Todd and Brant eating? What were they saying? Could they go to the toilet? And the biggest question of all—would they actually make it out?

It was time to boost our coverage. Everything else would need to wait, including David Koch's recovery from Kokoda. I joined him for a late flight to

Tasmania. *Sunrise* was now committed until the end, whatever that end would be.

Tuesday morning's show contained more detail than Monday's, thanks in part to the then national secretary of the Australian Workers' Union, Bill Shorten. Like Mel, he came to Beaconsfield on a private jet, but his plane was supplied by his friend Richard Pratt. Shorten says that that allowed him to be with his union members as quickly as possible. It's also true that had he taken a commercial flight, he would have missed that morning's television and radio shows.

Shorten went from reporter to reporter, and then back again. We spoke to him no fewer than four times that morning. Each interview started with a generic question like 'What are you hearing now?' Of course, he'd been too busy doing media interviews to have heard anything at all, but he knew what we needed. 'Look, it's certainly tense, but Australia stands behind Todd, Brant and the people of Beaconsfield.' He found different ways of saying that each time. Shorten impressed us all as good media talent. He was flexible and available, and would soon become the public voice of the miners. Here was a tough union official who could also show just the right level of emotion. Few doubted he would go far.

The growing media contingent was continuing to unnerve the locals. That wasn't helped by a producer from a tabloid current affairs show who was offering $10000 to any rescuer who'd smuggle a camera down the mine. It was standard operating procedure for him but seen as insulting by the community. He was soon frozen out.

There were two journalists in Beaconsfield who didn't raise any suspicion. It was immediately clear that David Koch and Melissa Doyle had a distinct advantage; *Sunrise* was easily the top rating breakfast show in Tasmania—but it was more than that. As Mel recalls, 'I think the locals knew us as people, rather than journos.' And that meant they were welcomed as friends, not seen as voyeurs. 'People would come and up and say hi,' says Mel, 'but I never wanted to assume they were a viewer in case I *did* actually know them, because people greeted us with such familiarity.' Such familiarity that one woman even followed Mel into a public toilet and waited outside the cubicle for a chat. 'I had to say to her, "Would you mind just waiting outside the block?"'

One newfound friend was Launceston paramedic Peter James, who'd been called to the mine for a critical mission. A small hole had been drilled into Todd and Brant's underground cage. Parts of a telephone were then dropped in for the pair to reassemble. That would become their lifeline to the outside world—or, at least, to Peter James. His job was to keep them talking, so that the underground silence wouldn't send them insane.

Before his first shift, Peter ran into Mel outside Beaconsfield's newsagent. He asked whether Kochie was around, revealing he was a massive fan. He also seized the opportunity to say: 'Mel, my wife thinks the world of you. Would you mind having a quick chat to her?' The paramedic then called home, putting Mel on the phone. That chance encounter would later serve *Sunrise* well.

By April 2006, Kochie and Mel were big network stars. Apart from *Sunrise,* they were also hosting the primetime reunion show *Where Are They Now?* The uplifting series had started only a few weeks earlier, so the breaking news from Beaconsfield was a major inconvenience for the show's producers. They needed the hosts back in Sydney on Tuesday afternoon, when two editions were due to be recorded. I agreed but on one condition—they'd need to be back in time for Wednesday's *Sunrise.* The only way the producers could make my deadline would be to charter a plane—and this time, on their dime, not mine. A private plane gave us a major advantage. Operation Dacien was about to begin.

Dacien Hadland is a television geek. He started working at Seven while finishing his Higher School Certificate in the year 2000. Then aged seventeen, his main job was to assist news producers. In his spare time, he taught himself to edit and one morning seized his chance when a *Sunrise* editor called in sick. His initiative impressed me and I kept him close to the show from that day on. Come 2006, Dacien had extraodinary insight into television production. He thought outside the box and for half the price. Forget the bureaucracy of our engineering department, he became our go-to guy to make things happen. When he jumped aboard Kochie and Mel's chartered jet, he was bringing more than a suitcase to Tasmania: he loaded up enough equipment to run a small TV station.

Seven now had no fewer than eight cameras in Beaconsfield capable of live coverage at any time of day, not just during *Sunrise.* Our cameras could see the mine, the church, the football oval, the main street and even the media compound itself. None of our rivals could match it.

We were making just as much progress across town, Kochie and Mel were busy making friends—more of them. Todd Russell's parents, Kaye and Noel, were born and bred in Beaconsfield. They lived on the main street, just a stone's throw from the mine. Since the news had broken that their son was alive, just about every journalist in town had knocked on their door. Some brought cameras, others brought a chequebook—but all were politely told to leave. When Kochie and Mel knocked, they were invited in for tea.

As hard as this might be to believe, the *Sunrise* hosts had no agenda other than to offer emotional support; they thought they could be a distraction from what was, no doubt, a tense and emotional time. And they were. So much so, that Kochie and Mel visited the Russells after every show in Beaconsfield. They'd talk about everything from television to the weather and, of course, Todd. Kaye firmly believed he'd be out soon enough. I joined them one morning when Kaye expressed concern about how Todd would handle the media attention once he got out. I suggested the family hire an agent who could then serve as a buffer. Despite the fact I knew he'd drain the networks of every last cent, I passed on a number for Harry M Miller. Harry had represented the survivor of the Thredbo landslide, Stuart Diver.

Harry later wrote in his autobiography: 'Kaye Russell called our office to ask for advice. At this stage, the two miners had been found but the rescue was still in progress. I decided to go to Beaconsfield. To this day, I remain amused that I was basically flying down for an audition.' It was an audition that didn't go well for Harry. The Russells didn't particularly like him and he didn't particularly like them. As he put it, 'While I appreciate the family was under serious strain, I felt as if they thought they already knew all the answers.'

On Thursday, 4 May, mine manager Matthew Gill delivered some positive news: he told a packed news conference that the boys could soon be out. A 16-metre pilot tunnel had just been completed, and would be used to guide a powerful machine that would eventually cut through the rock. They would start the process that night.

Every media outlet spent the night on standby. Up until then, many of us had been driving back to Launceston each night, to sleep in a hotel, which was risk-free, given the slow progress down the shaft. Matthew Gill's optimism meant we wouldn't be doing so that night: instead, journalists, cameramen and producers would be sleeping under the stars. We were excited about the story but fearful of the weather. Peter 'Zoomer' Morris had already slept on site and warned us that the after-dark chill was only part of the problem. 'Heavy, heavy rain,' he remembers. 'You could almost set your watch by it. It would hit around four in the morning and I'm talking a good hour's worth of rain.' Cold *and* wet. Wonderful. There was also hardly any room to move. Almost 200 members of the media were wedged into a small picnic area, right alongside the mine.

Bigger-name journalists were afforded the relative luxury of a Winnebago, about five of which had somehow been shoehorned into the area by the various broadcasters. Many of the cameramen set up camp underneath tarps, and wrapped battery packs around their chests in the hope it would keep them warm—workplace health and safety taking a back seat to practicality. Ever the boy scout, Dacien Hadland raided the local hardware and grocery stores for anything that could help. He brought back over-sized boots, garbage bags and even some sleeping bags. They had to be closely guarded.

At nightfall, Dacien, producer Rob McKnight and I sought shelter in the back of a small truck we'd been using as our camera control room. A complicated web of cables meant we couldn't close the truck's door.

We tried our best to sleep, but there was a problem that no amount of jumpers or pillows could ease. A junior audio technician had volunteered to stay awake in case anything happened at the mine. Every time one of us rolled over, we were confronted by him watching us sleep. It wasn't a casual glance—more an obsessive stare—and he was sitting right alongside us. I was relieved when the 4am rain woke the rest of the camp.

The night came and went without any breakthrough. As Bill Shorten did his morning round of interviews, he revealed he'd rather pick a winner for the Melbourne Cup than say when Todd and Brant would be free. Kochie and Mel again had morning tea with Kaye and Noel Russell, who weren't as disheartened as you might think. They pointed out they'd rather wait for a safe rescue than rush a dangerous one.

But frustration was setting in at the media compound: progress was just too slow beneath the ground. The media monster needed feeding and it had a whiff of something brewing. Questions were starting to emerge over the safety record of the Beaconsfield mine. Was an earthquake really to blame for the mine collapse?

Veteran *60 Minutes* reporter Richard Carleton brought the matter to a head, at a packed media conference on Sunday, 7 May. He asked mine manager Matthew Gill: 'On the twenty-sixth of October last year, not ten metres from where these men are now entombed, you had a 400-tonne rock fall. Why is it, is it the strength of the seam, or the wealth of the seam, that you continue to send men into work in such a dangerous environment?'

Just moments later, Carleton stepped away from the media pack and collapsed. Government media adviser Shaun Rigby shouted, 'He's down!' but few realised what he meant. As the media conference continued in the background, a Tasmanian radio reporter started CPR. Journalists kept firing questions at Gill, unaware of what was happening just ten metres away. I was with David Koch, up on a hill overlooking the scene. We could tell that someone was on the ground, but didn't know why.

People watching the media conference in Seven's Sydney control room also noticed a commotion. They asked Peter Morris to take a look. 'I was co-ordinating the live coverage of the media conference,' remembers Zoomer. 'I radioed back to Sydney that "It looks like someone has collapsed," and I walked over. I then said, "It's Richard Carleton, and he's not breathing." Craig Pickersgill heard that message from the media compound and immediately ran over.' Pickersgill was Seven's technical director and was trained in first aid. He assisted the radio reporter by providing chest compressions on Carleton, while others called for an ambulance.

Explains Zoomer: 'I was in a real predicament. Someone in Sydney was asking for a live shot of what was happening to Richard. I replied, "Trust me, you don't want to see what's going on here." So, instead, I asked for another cameraman to just record the scene without sending anything back live. I told him to shoot wide with no close-up shots. But even then, that material never got to air. We destroyed the footage.'

Members of the media, including Carleton's Channel Nine colleague Tracy Grimshaw, held up a wall of blankets around him. By the time the ambulance arrived, it was clear little more could be done. Carleton had died from a heart attack.

The media compound fell quiet. We especially felt for his many friends from Channel Nine; their shock was tangible. And his death served as a leveller for us all. As Zoomer puts it, 'It reminded everybody there of the frailty of life.' Just hours earlier, Carleton had been signing autographs for local kids. He wrote on one girl's piece of paper, 'Have a healthy life.'

Later that day, the media had little choice but to get back to work, having had word the underground rescuers were about to make their final push. Much of the rock blocking them from reaching Todd and Brant had now been removed. Their release was surely just days away. As good as that news was, it created a problem for *Sunrise* and one that was entirely removed from events in Beaconsfield.

In May 2004, a teenage boy in Victoria had taken the extraordinary step of 'divorcing' his mother. He argued the two would never get along and successfully applied for the Department of Human Services to become his legal guardian. Melbourne's *Herald Sun* newspaper reported the case in June 2004 and was soon followed by *Seven News, Today Tonight* and then *Sunrise.* It was one of those yarns that generate interest for twenty-four hours and then disappear off the radar.

It came as a surprise then when, almost a year later, detectives from the Victoria Police arrived at Channel Seven in Sydney, seeking to interview the executive producer of *Today Tonight,* Craig McPherson, and me. We were later charged with identifying parties who were appearing before the Children's Court—a serious offence that carries a maximum penalty of two years in jail. That was bad enough but, as the police were clearly out to set an example, they later increased the number of people charged to include Melissa Doyle, Natalie Barr and David Koch. They now had a high-profile case.

The hearing was set to begin in the Melbourne Magistrates' Court on Monday, 8 May. I flew to Melbourne before Monday's *Sunrise,* for an early meeting with Seven's lawyers. The plan was for Kochie and Mel to fly up after the show. We had little choice but to leave Beaconsfield; the charges were serious and needed defending. Then, as Kochie and Mel were driving to Launceston Airport, Mel called me. She was crying: 'We can't leave. We just can't leave until this story is over. I need it to end before I can leave town.' Their daily encounters with the Russells had weighed heavily on her. At one point that week, Mel and Kochie were inside a lift at their Launceston hotel when she collapsed into his arms and then totally lost it.

They were both too invested to just get up and go, so I told them to stay and I would cover for them in Melbourne. Keeping them there was one of the best decisions I ever made.

The following morning, Mel was asleep in her Launceston hotel when her phone rang just after 3am. It was her friend the paramedic, Peter James. 'It's happening. The boys will be out in a few hours.' Nobody else in the media had been told. Mel quickly woke the Channel Seven team. 'I didn't know whether to clean my teeth,' laughs Zoomer. 'I remember jumping around the room with one leg in one side of my jeans. I couldn't get dressed quickly enough. We all piled into this hire car and hightailed it.'

When they arrived at Beaconsfield, they tiptoed around the media compound, careful not to wake our competitors. Dacien Hadland placed a discreet call to Channel Seven's operations centre in Melbourne: 'Be ready to switch all programming to us at 4am.'

Everyone was in position. All eight cameras were manned. Dacien and producer Stuart Wallace were in the truck-cum-control room. With ten minutes to go, Craig Pickersgill fired up our generators. He waited until the last possible moment, because they'd serve as an alarm clock to the rest of the compound. Our bright broadcast lights flickered on.

At exactly 4am, Kochie and Mel were on the air. 'Good morning from Beaconsfield, where we can report some major breaking news. Todd Russell and Brant Webb are about to be freed from their underground cage. They will leave the mine this morning.'

Phones started ringing all over the media campsite. Dazed journalists were trying to work out what was happening. How did Channel Seven know about this? Some called it the scoop of the year.

Mel's early-morning tip-off wasn't the only inside information we had. Just before going on air, Kochie also received a call from Peter James. He told him that Todd wanted to see him when he emerged from down below, or, as Todd himself put it, 'Tell that fat, ugly bastard Kochie, I want him at the gate when we come out, so I can say g'day.' Like his parents, Todd was a big *Sunrise* fan, often watching the show after knocking off from his overnight shift at the mine. It was a love that had even spread to a third generation: when Todd's son won a book prize at school, he chose *Kochie's Best Jokes.* Peter James had conspired with Todd to keep the door of the ambulance open when it drove by the media, specifically so he could make contact with Kochie. We didn't really know what to expect, but placed extra cameras on stand-by.

Just after 5am, the old bells atop Beaconsfield's Uniting Church rang out across the town. They hadn't been heard since 1945, when they marked the end of the Second World War. Now, they signalled the end of a fourten-day ordeal. Locals converged on the mine, happy that two of their own were safe. Millions of people were glued to their televisions. Every station was showing the rescue—but most viewers were watching *Sunrise.*

At 5.54am, Todd and Brant entered the lift, to be pulled up by the poppet head and back into natural light. And, at 5.59am on Tuesday, 9 May, it happened: Todd Russell and Brant Webb walked out of the mine, punching the air. They were free and back in the arms of their families.

Cheering erupted around the mine and, no doubt, around Australia. I jumped with excitement inside my Melbourne hotel room. Mel, too, couldn't hold in her emotions. She told me recently: 'I remember crying and having a moment inside me saying, "Oh my God, I've just broken a cardinal rule as a journalist, you can't show emotion, you can't be that close," but, you know what, I'm a person. I hold dear to myself that I still have those feelings. If I stood up in a similar situation today and didn't have those emotions, then I think it would be time to give up my job.'

Todd and Brant were helped into two separate ambulances for the drive from the mine. Police had warned the media to keep its distance. Kochie and Mel waved as the ambulances went by but then, suddenly, one stopped. Todd was yelling at Kochie to run over. He did just that and then actually jumped into the ambulance. 'And as I did so,' recalls Kochie,

'I could hear producer Stuart Wallace through my earpiece, yelling, "Oh fuck. Oh fuck, he's not? He's getting into the ambulance!" Well, what was I meant to do?'

I almost fainted while watching this play out on live television, across all networks. Todd reached up and gave Kochie his miner's identification tag—it was a defining moment for *Sunrise* and for Kochie himself. And it wasn't just shown in Australia: international news channels were taking a live feed from Channel Seven. Kochie's daughter Samantha was working at Bloomberg in Hong Kong that morning, and he chuckles as he recalls, 'All of her colleagues looked at her in bewilderment when my arse filled the screen.'

Not knowing the backstory, the rest of the Australian media cried foul; Channel Nine even made a commercial that labelled *Sunrise* 'ambulance chasers'. Some of our viewers were also upset, emailing their complaints. Kochie and Mel dealt with the issue on the following morning's show.

> Kochie: So, I got into the ambulance and that's when he gave me his miner's tag. I got to say, a moment and a symbol I will cherish forever. And I make no apologies for that.

> Mel: 'Koch going into the ambulance is perhaps one of the most disgusting things I have ever witnessed on television. Is he more important

than the miners? I can't understand his ego. An apology from Koch would be useful.'

Kochie: Hmm, who is it from?

Mel: David in Tasmania.

Kochie: Well, David, you'll be waiting a long time if you want an apology. Look, I'm a boofhead sometimes, but I'm not a big enough boofhead that I'd jump a fence and jump into an ambulance uninvited. This was a bloke who had his life on the line for two weeks. If he wants me to cross the line, I'll cross it.

Peter Meakin agrees. He tells me now: 'The controversy was the biggest load of nonsense I'd ever heard in my life. Any journalist worth his salt would have leapt in the back.'

One former journalist knew exactly how significant that moment was. Eddie McGuire had just become the chief executive of Channel Nine and, as he watched Kochie getting into the ambulance, he figured, as we did, that Seven was well ahead in the race to snare the first big interview with Todd and Brant.

That night, he turned up in Beaconsfield. He walked into the Club Hotel with a big announcement: 'I am coming out of retirement to host one more *Footy Show* here in Beaconsfield. Free drinks on me!' There were cheers all round. It was a smart move. The man who'd soon be negotiating for rights to the interview was now the town's best mate; he wasn't a cold television executive, he was Eddie from *The Footy Show* and an all-round good bloke.

Eddie hosted the joint NRL and AFL edition of the show on Thursday, 11 May, live from the Beaconsfield Town Hall. Todd's a mad AFL fan and Brant loves the NRL, and Eddie convinced the pair to be part of the show, as a way of thanking their rescuers. How could they say no?

The men didn't want to say much about their ordeal, but Eddie tried anyway.

> Eddie: Todd, I've gotta ask you, though—I'd be sacked as the journo—I'd have to front the CEO tomorrow if I didn't ask you a question about what it was like down in that mine.
>
> Todd: Listen, mate—tell me how big your chequebook is and we'll talk.
>
> Brant: Fair call.

Eddie laughed and the crowd cheered. The terms were now clear for everyone.

Some observers felt that the miners' appearance on *The Footy Show* devalued any potential deal. McGuire himself dismissed that, by telling the *Age:* 'To be perfectly honest, their appearance shows what ripping blokes they are. In the past, we've seen people go from hero to zero in these bidding wars. These blokes are just normal blokes.' He was right. Todd and Brant were set to cash in.

David Koch's manager, Sean Anderson, was appointed by the families to represent them, on the recommendation of Kochie himself. Higher-profile agents like Harry M Miller and Max Markson returned to the mainland. In the end, Kochie's connection to Anderson meant little; a lawyer by trade, Anderson knows how to cement the best possible deal.

Seven and Nine were well aware that exclusivity wouldn't come cheap. Behind the scenes, both reached out to their sister companies, in the hope they could share the financial burden. In the case of Nine, the miners would be required to do not just a television interview but follow-up stories with ACP Magazines.

Anderson called Nine's negotiator, Jeffrey Browne, who is said then to have offered $2.5 million and given Anderson just ten seconds to accept. He counted down over the phone: ten, nine, eight ... When he reached three seconds, Anderson agreed but with one condition—he'd need to get sign-off from Todd and Brant.

As further evidence of the strength of their relationship, Todd then called David Koch. He wanted to make sure that Kochie was fine with him jumping into bed with Channel Nine. Kochie told him that it was a once-in-a-lifetime opportunity and that he should do what was best for his family. Todd and

Brant then consented to the most expensive interview in Australian media history.

Despite Kochie's grace in handling this conversation, there is little doubt we were bitterly disappointed. We'd owned this story from start to finish. We'd worked our contacts, befriended the town and provided daily coverage that was second-to-none. All that was left was the big tell-all interview. Without a chequebook, it would have been ours. I think Nine would have paid just about anything to deprive us of that prize, though. It wasn't just a question of pride. Here was a new chief executive out to prove he could get things done. McGuire proudly boasted, 'People know when big stories happen, the place to be is Nine.' Well, at least for one night. Tracy Grimshaw's interview with Todd and Brant was watched by almost three million people.

Despite losing the bidding war, *Sunrise* didn't lose its connection with the people of Beaconsfield. We returned with some of Australia's biggest names on 17 May. It was our way of saying thanks: thanks for putting up with the media, thanks for sharing your spirit and thanks for the exceptional beef pies! Our special three-hour broadcast included, sadly, one of Steve Irwin's final public appearances. It was a special morning that attracted people from throughout the Tamar Valley.

Beaconsfield was so much more than just another story. As then opposition leader Kim Beazley put it,

'Everybody became a citizen of Beaconsfield, every single Australian became a citizen of Beaconsfield in the course of those two weeks.' It certainly felt like that to us.

We left Beaconsfield with one loose end: it was finally time to face the music in a Melbourne court. Had we broken the law by talking about the teenager who'd divorced his mum? Magistrate Lisa Hannan ruled we hadn't. In dismissing the charges, she agreed we'd only discussed the case in a general way, as opposed to specifically reporting on a proceeding in the Children's Court.

Kochie, Mel and I didn't say much on the flight to Sydney, on our way back from something that marked the end of three weeks we'll never forget and a turning point for the show. We now knew our actions had consequences—and not just in law. We'd seen our influence in Beaconsfield and the impact we had on our viewers. We'd weathered the sting of criticism and the jealousy of our opponents.

We'd become more than a daggy little breakfast show. *Sunrise* now made news, instead of just reporting it.

10

'THE SUNLIES AFFAIR'

It was Easter Sunday 2007 and Kevin Rudd was about to blow a gasket.

'Have you seen today's *Sunday Telegraph?*'

I hadn't. I was still asleep when he called, just before 5am.

'What the fuck are they talking about?'

The paper's front page screamed, 'Rudd's Anzac Insult.' Political reporter Linda Silmalis had written, 'Vietnam veterans have been offended by Labor Leader Kevin Rudd's request for a fake Dawn Service so he can commemorate Anzac Day live on Channel Seven's *Sunrise* breakfast show from Long Tan in Vietnam.' The story seemed to come out of nowhere and, with a federal election due later that year, the now opposition leader was understandably upset. He told me: 'I'm going to sue them. I'm going to fucking sue them.'

Like Rudd, it never crossed my mind that the story had any substance, so I headed straight for work, to write a strong denial to air on our Sunday morning show, *Weekend Sunrise.* Lisa Wilkinson was the program's co-host and told our audience that 'the facts have been overshadowed for the sake of a good headline'. With the denial, I wasn't just defending Kevin Rudd, I was defending our show. Later that day, Rudd issued an equally unequivocal statement: 'Neither I, nor anyone from my office, has spoken to or had any conversation with anyone whatsoever about requesting the changing of a Dawn Service time at Long Tan in Vietnam or anywhere else.' These defiant words from both Rudd and me would put us on a collision course with not only the might of News Limited but also an increasingly desperate federal government. Neither of us could foresee the toll that would soon take.

But, to fully understand this story, we first need to go back to December 2006 and the Kokoda Track trek. After being so moved by it, David Koch vowed to visit other theatres of war and, in particular, ones he felt hadn't been given their rightful attention. He introduced me to Vietnam veteran Kerry Phelan, who was keen to have *Sunrise* retrace the route an Australian regiment had taken leading up to the Battle of Long Tan.

Phelan was just twenty years old when he was called up for national service in 1966. He had grown up on a farm in Western Australia, and Vietnam wasn't a place he knew much about. He touched down at a place called Vũng Tàu, where he took up duties as a driver. He remembers being thankful that he wasn't required to walk the jungles at night. One day, he was part of a convoy on its way to an Australian base in Nui Dat. A Vietnamese teenager on a motorbike got in their path and ended up being flung under the truck Phelan was driving. The convoy was travelling at high speed in order to deliver urgent supplies, so there was no time to stop. Phelan isn't sure what happened to the teenager, but the accident haunts him to this day.

During his twelve months of service in Vietnam, he was always on edge. He'd carry a gun even going to the toilet. He knew of too many people who'd been struck down while not watching their back. His vigilance continued after he got back to Australia. Like most veterans, he wasn't offered counselling; he just had to resume work. Feeling vulnerable even today, he hates using ATMs and prefers to sit in the corners of restaurants. Phelan also feels a deep sadness about the suffering the people of Vietnam endured because of the war, and played an active part in raising money for a kindergarten that now stands on the site of an old Australian base.

I met Phelan in a conference room at Channel Seven. He spoke in a humble, matter-of-fact way. As I listened, I felt embarrassed by how little I knew about the Vietnam War and, especially, the bravery of the Australians who served. Nothing typifies that more than the Battle of Long Tan. Early in the morning of 17 August 1966, members of 'D Company' walked into a rubber plantation near Long Tan, only to come under heavy machine-gun fire from the Viet Cong. They were quickly surrounded, just 105 Australians up against an enemy of at least 2000. For three hours, they endured heavy fighting before reinforcements came to their aid. While eighteen Australians were killed, it's remarkable the toll wasn't higher. Against all odds, they'd held off a major ambush. Phelan wanted other Australians to see where that battle took place. I told him we'd do all we could to make that happen.

Sunrise producer Paula Crawford (who'd worked on our Kokoda project) was assigned to start looking into the logistics. We wanted to time the expedition to end at Long Tan on Anzac Day 2007. The Australian consulate in Ho Chi Minh City gave positive feedback. We again extended invites both to Kevin Rudd and Joe Hockey. Rudd accepted but Hockey already had other commitments, so Bronwyn Bishop volunteered to go instead.

As with Kokoda, the plan was to broadcast a live service during the show (this time without the offensive shirts) but time differences meant it couldn't be the Dawn Service. Kerry Phelan assured us there was a simple yet still meaningful alternative. As he explained to the *Australian* newspaper: 'Usually when we get to Long Tan, we pay a silent tribute. Individuals present themselves at the cross, bow their head and spend a moment in reflection.' In other words, something very different from a traditional Dawn Service.

But that didn't mean the official service was completely off our radar. In talks with the Australian consulate, Paula Crawford asked who'd be attending it in case it was worth inviting them on our show, which is what a good producer does. In a case of Chinese whispers, that conversation was somehow relayed to retired brigadier Bill Rolfe, who worked at the Department of Veterans' Affairs in Canberra. Rolfe, himself a Vietnam veteran, became convinced that *Sunrise* wanted to change the timing of the official service, and if that wasn't possible, stage a fake Dawn Service to suit our broadcast times. That was never the case: we never asked for that, nor did anyone in Kevin Rudd's office. Kerry Phelan confirms, 'We were going to film a tribute and get the cameras out of there before the official Dawn Service began.'

Bill Rolfe wasn't someone we'd heard of and certainly wasn't someone who had anything to do with our plans for Long Tan. Maybe that's why we didn't rush to get back to him when he contacted us on 22 March, seeking a meeting. A week later, he'd become frustrated that we hadn't replied. He called Channel Seven and was put through to Paula. Her offer to call him back and have a more detailed chat left him far from impressed. He accused her of being more interested in heading to after-work drinks than in listening to the concerns of a veteran.

Paula is one of the hardest-working people I know. Not trained as a journalist or producer, she got her start in the newsroom as Ian Cook's assistant and had to put in twice the effort to prove herself in a producing role. And, to me, she was doing exactly that. Her exchange with Rolfe left her almost in tears. I sent him an impulsive email: 'Rather than knocking off to "indulge in a few reds" as you so confidently suggest, Paula is off to get some sleep. Because of a ferry accident in Sydney last night, she has been working since midnight.'

I wasn't done.

'I'm not sure if you're aware of what we do here—but essentially, we connect Australian audiences to moments of significance ... Our broadcast last year from Kokoda was praised by Government ministers and many, many veterans. We're proposing to do something similar this year from Vietnam. Do we have a problem?'

Rolfe wrote back the next day, firstly to apologise for his attack on Crawford, and then to state his concerns. 'I have a problem with the conduct of a pretend Dawn Service at 0400 hours on Anzac Day ... That's my problem—as both a Vietnam veteran and as a person vitally interested in the powerful tradition of the Dawn Service.'

Around the same time, he sent a similar email to Kevin Rudd's personal secretary, Mary Mawhinney. In it, he echoed his complaint about what he perceived to be a fake Dawn Service, telling her, 'I would see some danger in such an action seriously offending veterans and perhaps the wider community.' It seems

Mawhinney never shared those concerns with Rudd himself.

I was bemused by Rolfe's assumptions. Our planned tribute was never going to resemble a full service and, in fact, would take place well before the sun rose over Vietnam. I responded to him, explaining that. My email ended with me clearly assuring Rolfe, 'We won't call it a Dawn Service.' I thought the matter was settled when he sent one final email: 'I do not begrudge you for your approach. I will assist where I can but I will still conduct an official ceremony at dawn.' We saw no reason why he shouldn't. That was the last time anyone at *Sunrise* dealt with Rolfe. Then, on Easter Sunday, the *Sunday Telegraph* shocked us all with its sensational front page.

Rudd felt comfortable vehemently denying the story. First, he had never asked for a fake Dawn Service, as the paper had claimed. Second, he was convinced that nobody in his office knew of any such plans. And, third, he fully understood the difference between a Dawn Service and a silent tribute.

He was determined to be vindicated.

In 2007, Jane Summerhayes was an in-house lawyer at News Limited. She'd arranged an Easter lunch at her place for some of her colleagues—mainly those without a lot of family in Sydney. *Sunday Telegraph* editor Neil Breen arrived to see his deputy, Helen McCabe, looking worried. McCabe was on the phone, but covered it with her hand to whisper to Breen, 'There's drama. We have drama.'

Breen wasn't too concerned. There's always drama when you run one of the biggest papers in the country. He went and got himself a drink. Then his own phone rang. It was David Penberthy, editor of Breen's sister paper the *Daily Telegraph:* 'Mate, Rudd is going ballistic.' He then described an extraordinary conversation he'd just had with the opposition leader. According to Penberthy, Rudd complained: 'the *Sunday Telegraph* makes up these fucking lies and puts them on page one. As a result of your papers, fifteen million people around the country think I'm a fucking cunt.' Penberthy and Breen chuckled about Rudd's overly kind assessment of their circulation figures. They both felt he would eventually calm down, so Breen went back to the lunch.

On the other side of town, David Koch was at a lunch of his own. He was as upset as Rudd, knowing that our Anzac Day plan was meant to honour Vietnam veterans, not offend them. We feared that *Sunrise* viewers would be questioning our integrity, particularly on the back of the controversy over shirts at Kokoda.

I did what I could to brief journalists on what we knew to be the real story. Koch, in the meantime, worked on an email to members of the *Sunrise* family, which probably numbered a few hundred thousand at the time. It went out just before sunset on Easter Sunday: 'Perhaps like you, I woke this morning to see the headline that we're somehow trying to undermine the Anzac spirit, by staging our own Dawn Service in Vietnam for Kevin Rudd's benefit. I couldn't believe it. The story was totally from left field.'

Koch, Rudd and I maintained our defence: The *Sunday Telegraph* story was false.

On Tuesday morning, Rudd called News Limited's chief executive, John Hartigan. He was still raging after Sunday and wanted a public apology. Hartigan wasn't prepared to offer that—but he did quiz Neil Breen who revealed that his reporter, Linda Silmalis, had based her story on the email trail between Bill Rolfe, Paula Crawford, Kevin Rudd's secretary and me. She didn't have actual copies of the emails; her source had read them to her over the phone. 'We had a story involving the biggest TV show in the morning and the guy who was going to be prime minister. It had all the sexy elements,' Breen says.

Rudd was worried the Anzac story could damage him in an upcoming opinion poll, so thought it was time to bring matters to a head. On Thursday, 12 April, he again called John Hartigan, insisting he put out a statement apologising both to him and *Sunrise* by 1pm. He didn't say what would happen if that ultimatum wasn't met.

Hartigan was still backing his editor, but warned him that now was the time to cover his bases. Breen called a meeting with his paper's senior staff. 'I told them that we need hard copies of those emails today or we're stuffed. We just had to get them.' Linda Silmalas called her source, saying that she was about to take a major hit, unless she had the emails. The source refused to email them, from fear of being exposed, but arranged for them to be faxed.

It was 12.45pm.

Deputy editor Helen McCabe prepared a briefing note for Hartigan, outlining exactly who said what. The News Limited boss was satisfied the story was solid. At 1pm, he picked up the phone to Kevin Rudd. He wanted Breen to stay in his office to hear his opening line: 'Kevin, I'm afraid you've just wasted five days of my time.' After enduring what he calls 'the most intense pressure I have been under in my journalistic career', Breen was ready to deliver the knockout punch. He took the emails down to David Penberthy at the *Daily Telegraph,* who was in a meeting but promised to read them later.

Now reeling from news that his office had in fact been told about the concerns from veterans, Rudd extended an olive branch. He invited Breen down to Sydney's InterContinental Hotel for coffee. Breen tells me the encounter was anything but comfortable as Rudd, too late, tried his best to retreat from his original position.

As Rudd and Breen were talking, David Penberthy was on the roof of News Limited's Sydney headquarters, reading the email chain while having a cigarette. As soon as he was done, he sent Breen a text: 'Hey mate, we are smashing [Rudd] on the front page tomorrow.' Penberthy sent that text to Rudd by mistake. Immediately realising what he'd done, he sent him another text addressed to journalist Kelvin Bissett, in the hope of creating the impression that both were meant for Kelvin and not Kevin. Rudd knew it was pointless to complain. He was about to be slammed—it was just a question of how hard.

Friday's *Daily Telegraph* went for the jugular with a front-page headline that screamed 'I'm with stupid', above a photo of Kevin Rudd pointing at David Koch. For the next forty-eight hours, we waged an unwinnable battle as every Murdoch paper opened fire. They accused *Sunrise* of stamping on the graves of diggers to satisfy our thirst for ratings.

Kochie was particularly hurt by the coverage. He walked into my office on Friday morning and wondered aloud whether it was time to throw in the towel. 'What's the point of trying to do something good if we're just going to be accused of the opposite? Maybe we shouldn't even try.'

I assured him that we'd get through it but, deep down, I was just as shaken. My first, angry, email to Bill Rolfe had been printed for all to see. The tone was perceived as arrogant, and talkback callers were accusing me of having no respect for veterans.

The Howard government joined the fray. There's little doubt that someone from within the Coalition was responsible for the leaks to Linda Silmalis; here was a chance to embarrass the man causing them so much pain. Then foreign minister Alexander Downer (who we privately blamed) declared, 'This just confirms the political opportunism of Kevin Rudd.' Then health minister Tony Abbott said to the media, 'Kevin really needs to explain himself here.'

Rudd tried to do just that, by releasing a backtracking statement: 'My staff have informed me that in their search of the documentary record on Easter Sunday, the email (from Bill Rolfe) was overlooked. I have now counselled my staff on this matter.' That didn't ease the pressure—the Coalition mantra became 'If he can't run his office, then he can't run the country.' The lone government voice defending both Rudd and *Sunrise* was show regular Joe Hockey. He was later chastised by colleagues for saying, 'No one should in any way doubt the intentions of *Sunrise,* of Adam Boland, of Kochie or Kevin Rudd.'

We knew the worst was yet to come; the *Sunday Telegraph* had waited a week to have its say. As Melissa Doyle puts it: 'There's nothing worse than feeling this avalanche rolling down the hill, knowing you have absolutely no control over it. There's nothing you can say or do to make it okay.' The Sunday tabloid dedicated not only the front page but also four inside pages to what it dubbed 'The Sunlies Affair'. Neil Breen's editorial showed no mercy: 'By Thursday, when the *Sunday Telegraph* produced email evidence and presented it to Mr Rudd—*Sunrise* and Seven were exposed as liars. For a show, and for a network, whose duty is to inform the public in a balanced matter, there is no worse offence.' He saved his most savage jibe for me: 'Boland began the week gleefully issuing statements about how wrong this newspaper was. He rightly finished the week worried about his ongoing employment.'

I read those words just before 1am on Sunday. I'd driven to innercity Kings Cross, to pick up an early edition of the paper. I couldn't sleep, so figured I should just face the inevitable. I sat in my car and cried. In my mind, I'd done nothing wrong, but now my show and my career were both crumbling.

I offered my resignation to Kerry Stokes, David Leckie and Peter Meakin. All three rejected it. The following day, Meakin told the media, 'Any suggestion that Boland's career is in jeopardy is a load of nonsense.' That was good of him, but I knew I'd let the network down. And, even worse, I'd let down David Koch and Kerry Phelan; a simple chain of emails had undermined their genuine effort to do something they cared deeply about. I went back to work and pulled the pin on our trip to Vietnam. If it went ahead, the negative media attention would have overshadowed Phelan's original goals. He told me he understood, and even continued to defend us in public: 'People have got this notion that Channel Seven was going to hijack the service. That is fundamentally wrong.'

Seven years on, Breen counsels me: 'You were a victim of the government's desperation. After ten years of Coalition rule, it was all going to end because of this guy from Queensland, Kevin Rudd. And they didn't know how to stop him. So when something like this came along, they were always going to exploit it.'

That wouldn't have happened, though, if I'd simply picked up the phone to Bill Rolfe when he first contacted my office. Not having done so is something I will always regret. Also, these days I'm much more careful about what I write in emails.

News Limited wasn't the only outlet using our own emails to hang us. Our television rivals joined in, as did countless blogs. We were also swamped with angry letters from disappointed *Sunrise* viewers. Many vowed never to watch us again. Anyone who stopped to actually read the emails in context would have seen there was no plan for us to cover a Dawn Service—fake or otherwise. But politics is all about perception.

A fortnight after the original *Sunday Telegraph* story, Kevin Rudd and Joe Hockey put an end to their weekly *Sunrise* segment. For five years, they'd offered our viewers a direct line to those with power. It had proved a game-changing segment that made politics accessible. Both Rudd and Hockey said their decision had nothing to do with the Anzac furore but, as I'd learned, the truth can be irrelevant.

11

DARKEST BEFORE THE DAWN

Beijing's Summer Palace—once a place for emperors to enjoy the spoils of their 'Mandate of Heaven'. During a visit there in May 2007, I discovered my own empire was under attack.

Production manager Dave Masala and I were in China to find broadcast locations for the Olympic Games. Back in Sydney, *Weekend Sunrise* host Lisa Wilkinson was being wined and dined by Channel Nine boss Jeffrey Browne and the network's head of news and current affairs, Garry Linnell. She called me soon afterwards. 'I know you're in China, but I didn't want you to read about it in the papers.' Whenever a phone call starts like that, you know it's not going to end well.

Lisa began hosting *Weekend Sunrise* at its inception in April 2005. She'd been a regular guest on *Sunrise* before that and always struck us as someone who should be doing a whole lot more. She made the weekend role her own, easily navigating both tough interviews and light banter. No surprise then that Channel Nine thought she'd be an ideal recruit. Eddie

McGuire was the first to approach her, in 2006, but she still had a year to run on her contract at Seven. Come 2007, she put me on notice that she was craving to do more than a single day of television a week (Weekend Sunrise didn't run on both Saturdays and Sundays until almost three years later). We didn't want to lose her but there was no way we were going to bump Mel Doyle from Sunrise.

We still had one thing up our sleeve. We'd just won approval for a new mid-morning show that would run straight after Sunrise each day. It would have a lighter magazine format than the breakfast show, but would still offer the energy and unpredictability of live television. Before flying to China, I sat down with Lisa at the same place Rudd and Hockey once enjoyed their weekly breakfasts: the inner-city Bond Café. I walked her through the format of what we'd creatively dubbed The Morning Show. Lisa was honest: it wasn't for her. She'd hosted an advertorial-based show once before (Seven's The Morning Shift in 2000, alongside Duncan Armstrong) and she didn't fancy a return to that stye of television. She wanted to get her teeth stuck into meatier content.

The phone call in China therefore wasn't entirely unexpected. She told me she would replace Jessica Rowe as host of Today at the end of the month (Jessica and Karl Stefanovic had taken over from Tracy Grimshaw and Steve Liebmann during Today's downward spiral in 2005). As Lisa later told the media, 'When Channel Nine suggested doing what I love five days a week, instead of just one, it was, ultimately, impossible to refuse.'

The deal with Nine was done so quickly that Lisa hadn't even met her soon-to-be co-host, Karl Stefanovic, before her new role was splashed across the Sunday tabloids. That made for a rather awkward encounter later that night, at television's Logie Awards in Melbourne. Lisa was chatting to game show king Larry Emdur when Karl happened to wander by. 'Oh, Karl,' Larry called out. 'Meet your new co-host, Lisa Wilkinson.'

Initially, I considered Lisa's defection a betrayal. I felt that without us putting her in the *Weekend Sunrise* chair, Nine would never have courted her. David Koch was just as upset. Only a matter of weeks earlier, we'd held a major think-tank on the future of *Sunrise* to which she had been party. He couldn't believe she'd sat through that knowing she was likely to jump ship. The selfish nature of our responses demonstrates how passionate we were about the show and the value we placed on loyalty. You never cross the family. The fact I would do that very thing six years later would have been impossible for me even to contemplate back then.

Losing Lisa did have one upside. Rather than just trying to satisfy a restless host, we could now give greater thought to who should present *The Morning Show*. Adding a 9am show to our daily line-up was, in many ways, a no-brainer. Even though *Sunrise* was at its peak (with an average viewing audience of 420000), we were facing a growing problem: our audience after eight-thirty each morning started to drop.

There was an obvious reason. The program that followed *Sunrise* was aimed at preschoolers. The network was obliged to run a certain amount of children's programming each day to satisfy regulatory requirements, but hardly any of our *Sunrise* viewers would stick around to watch it—in fact, 67 per cent just switched off. From a ratings point of view, it was as if the network jumped off a cliff each day at 9am.

Our competitors didn't have that problem because they chose to run their kids shows later. Channel Nine dominated the 9am slot, with Kerri-Anne Kennerley securing about 150000 viewers each day. Channel Ten's magazine show, *9am with David and Kim,* came in second, with about 120000 viewers, while Seven was a distant third. That was a spectacular turnaround from the breakfast slot, where *Sunrise* was unassailable. It was a bad day for us if our winning margin fell below 100000 viewers.

Mid-mornings weren't a priority for our network programmers (just like in 2002, when breakfast television wasn't seen as worthwhile). They didn't feel as strongly as the *Sunrise* team that the 9am slot was winnable, given there were already two established magazine shows. They were also loath to move the children's program to later in the day, in case it impacted on their late afternoon line-up that led into the all-important 6pm news.

Thankfully, though, we had an argument that was too strong to dismiss: revenue.

Nine's and Ten's morning shows both featured those long-winded commercials that flog everything from steak knives to wonder bras. Advertorials might be annoying to most but they're absolute cash cows to networks. The two networks were sharing around $30 million a year. Seven wasn't getting a cent. Seven's head of sales, James Warburton, thought that was nuts. His instruction to me was clear: 'You design the program and I'll make sure it gets on air.'

'Designing a show is always the fun bit. The 9am slot was so tired,' remembers former *Sunrise* producer Fiona Fagan. 'Kerri-Anne's show would often start with segments about shoes. New high heels or whatever. It was bizarre.' We wanted our show to have the same energetic feel as *Sunrise*. It needed to be fun but also full of sameday topics, to make it relevant. It would differ from our breakfast show in that interviews would get more time. There'd also be more lifestyle-based segments and a heavier emphasis on entertainment. Ultimately, however, the show's success would come down to the strength of the hosts and, in particular, their on-air chemistry.

Lisa's drinking companion at the Logies, Larry Emdur, was our early target. Even though he started his career reporting the news, he was best known as the ever-smiling host of shows like *The Price is Right* and *Wheel of Fortune.* But when *Wheel* was axed in late 2006, Larry was lost in the wilderness, telling the *Sydney Morning Herald* that 'I have done all the stuff I have really wanted to do and there is nothing jumping out at me in TV.' Channel Ten's popular talk show host Rove McManus was having none of it. He launched a tongue-in-cheek campaign to 'Save Larry Emdur' and even protested outside Channel Seven while *Sunrise* was on air.

Not long afterwards, we invited Larry to fill in for Lisa's former co-host on *Weekend Sunrise,* Andrew O'Keefe. He did so well that we asked him back, to cover for David Koch on *Sunrise.* He was both self-deprecating and genuinely interested in those he interviewed. Viewers gave him the thumbs up and so did we. He had no problems adapting to a different style of television. Just like with Lisa Wilkinson, though, we couldn't offer anything he wanted at the time he wanted. We were a full house. So, instead, he signed up to host a show called *Celebrity Dog School* on Channel Ten. It really was a dog of a show and was cancelled mid-season. That proved fateful for him and us. *The Morning Show* had just been green-lit. Larry agreed to host.

There were plenty of candidates to be his co-host. Some in the network actively pushed for Johanna Griggs. Other hopefuls came knocking on our door; every agent in town was sending us wine. Perhaps the only person who didn't ask for the gig was Kylie Gillies.

Kylie had long been restricted to reading news or sports updates. And that meant viewers hadn't *really* met her. Autocues never allow presenters to show their true personalities. Sometimes that's a good thing; I can think of plenty of people who should never leave home without one. But Kylie is not one of those people. We discovered more of Kylie 'the person' when she started presenting sports news on *Weekend Sunrise.* There's nowhere to hide sitting across the desk from Andrew O'Keefe. He lures everyone around him into the conversation. Kylie shone: she had views, she could joke around and, most importantly, she wasn't fake.

She had all the makings of a television star, but didn't know it. When we asked her to do a chemistry test with Larry, she was genuinely surprised. Just before her audition, she dropped by my office for advice. She was clearly nervous. I told her to be herself, which is often the one thing presenters struggle to be. From the moment she sat down, it was a done deal—Kylie and Larry had an instant rapport. To me, their different backgrounds would help sell the show. Kylie had come from the world of serious news, while Larry had mastered entertainment. If they could meet somewhere in the middle, we'd have one very appealing product.

They both embraced the format. They didn't take themselves too seriously and were excited about building something new. Unlike Kochie and Mel, they didn't get their own offices, but seemed perfectly happy sitting on the production desk alongside producers. They wanted to be part of every aspect of the show.

We used rehearsals to road-test new segments including live counselling sessions. Reality television was all the rage and it was clear that viewers enjoyed being voyeurs. I wanted to tap into that by using private problems as our everyday fodder. Fiona Fagan had produced many of the relationship-based segments on *Sunrise.* She had a knack for exploring all types of personal issues, from sex to divorce. She would have made a very good agony aunt. Given where I wanted to take the show, she struck me as the perfect person to be its editorial leader (she would later produce similar shows in London). Fiona felt confident that her team could find everyday Australians to share all on television. That kind of sharing had never been a problem for Americans, who had turned the likes of Jerry Springer into gods. We weren't planning live paternity tests or profiles of men who marry horses (once the topic of an entire *Springer* episode), but issues faced by people every day, such as tension over money or trouble with the in-laws.

We'd occasionally used a psychologist on *Sunrise,* who we knew could steer such segments with ease. Jo Lamble was forever warm and caring, with seemingly endless empathy. Some of our staff even used her as a shoulder to cry on. She worked so well in rehearsals for *The Morning Show* that we started to include her in publicity photos alongside Kylie and Larry. 'Real issues with real people' became our early slogan. That would surely prove more effective than segments about shoes.

Fiona also put together an extended team of regular guests to talk about everything from entertainment to beauty. The problem was, we gave her a relatively small budget or, as she puts it, 'a budget so tiny that it was almost impossible to do anything'. Most of the contributors agreed to appear for free, which would have been fine had it not been for our makeup room—always a hotbed of gossip. Word got around that some of the more high-profile members of the team were getting paid for every spot they did. 'We had a near mutiny on our hands,' recalls Fiona. In the end, we agreed to pay every regular the same flat fee.

There remained a bigger challenge, though: the inevitable dead weight of advertorials. We accepted they were a necessary evil but felt there had to be a better way than shouting for six minutes about a non-stick frying pan.

I was always a massive fan of Graham Kennedy—so much so, that just a few years earlier, I'd forked out more than $14000 to buy his old television crown. It was presented to Kennedy during his final episode of

In Melbourne Tonight in 1969, with newsreader Sir Eric Pearce declaring him the King of Australian Television. It was little more than a television prop consisting of a gold-coloured metal frame, some simulated pearls and a purple velvet cap. Kennedy clearly didn't care all that much about it. His old mate John Mangos once told me that he kept it under his bed with other things he considered junk, like Logies. A year after his death, the crown somehow ended up at an op shop. Someone paid just $5 for it, thinking his son might like it for dress-up day at school. When the man spotted the very same crown in old television footage, he knew he had something much more significant than a toy. It was verified by the Powerhouse Museum in Sydney and put up for auction. My bid earned the dad a pretty good return on his $5 investment. (I sold the crown in 2011, to raise money for victims of the Japanese tsunami. It's now kept at the National Film and Sound Archive in Canberra.)

Kennedy had his own unique approach to advertorials during the days of *In Melbourne Tonight.* One of the show's biggest sponsors was Pal dog food, and he thought it would be fun to involve his beloved Labrador, Rover, in the live commercial. The idea was simple enough: Kennedy would serve the dog a can of Pal before Rover licked the bowl clean. Delicious. Rover, though, opted to skip the food. Instead, Kennedy's massive television audience watched as the Labrador lifted his leg and pissed on a studio camera.

It was a classic television moment. So much so, that Rover became a star. Agent Harry M Miller negotiated an appearance fee for the dog: every time he was used, Pal would pay $500. Never one to miss an opportunity, Harry insisted on his standard 20 per cent. If Kennedy could make advertorials watchable back in the 1960s, why couldn't we, in 2007?

Rob McKnight was one of the most creative producers I knew. Having watched his work at both Seven's promos department and *Seven News,* I knew he thought outside the box. As we geared up to launch *The Morning Show,* Rob was working for Seven's production division on a reality show. He couldn't believe I would even consider asking him to turn his back on a top-rating performer in primetime to work on an unproven mid-morning show. But when I evoked the memory of Kennedy, his interest spiked; the bold assignment of making advertorials engaging was too good to turn down.

'The tricky bit wasn't so much making entertainment content,' says Rob. 'It was getting clients to take a leap of faith.' Advertisers told us they had a proven model; Snuggies and juice machines would fly out the door every time they ran spots on Kerri-Anne. We told them they'd sell twice as many if they allowed us to make their segments entertaining.

All was set for *The Morning Show* to debut on Monday, 18 June 2007.

That date also marked fifteen years since the death of Peter Allen, and we thought it would be a good idea to dedicate a chunk of our hour from 10am to celebrating his life. Todd McKenney played Allen in the hit stage show *The Boy from Oz,* so we booked him for both an interview and performance.

Two hours before the show, Todd called in sick. 'Fuck,' said Fiona Fagan. 'Why is this happening on our first show?'

Larry Emdur had the perfect solution: an SOS to our viewers. We used a Sydney radio station and *Sunrise* to issue a last-minute appeal to anyone who felt they could perform an Allen classic on live television. Our phones rang off the hook, turning a potential crisis into an unintentional publicity bonanza. Two sixteen-year-old Sydney schoolboys got the gig. Joel Newman played the piano while Alex Gibson-Giorgio sang—their rendition of 'Tenterfield Saddler' was a smash.

'That's the beauty of live television,' says Fiona. 'You never know where it's going to take you.' Nor did our clients. One of Rob McKnight's first advertorials featured presenter Glenn Wheeler dressed as a dust mite and being hung from wires. Kennedy would have been proud.

The team crowded around my computer screen at eight-thirty the following morning. Judgment time. We all wanted strong ratings but didn't expect to knock off Kerri-Anne any time soon. New shows take time to build.

The numbers were unbelievable. *The Morning Show* averaged 272000 viewers. Kerri-Anne was relegated to third position, with 126000. David and Kim on Channel Ten snuck into second place, with 147000. It was a stunning debut. And, from that point on, the show never lost a single day for years. Seven now owned breakfast and morning television.

I should have been over the moon. I'd been on a high leading up to the show's launch, flirting with media writers, signing off on sets and designing new segments. It was as if I didn't need sleep. But, suddenly, I struggled even to function.

I was also having regular panic attacks for no apparent reason. One of the worst came when I was in the middle of a busy shopping centre. Without any warning, I felt an overwhelming sense of being trapped. My breathing quickened and I could feel myself sweating. I just wanted to run and hide. I headed for the car park, careful to avoid eye contact with anyone. I feared I was about to implode and didn't want anyone to see. When I reached my car, I was too scared to drive. Instead, I just covered my face. If I couldn't see the world, then the world couldn't see me. It took me almost an hour to start the car.

I also didn't show my face at a ratings party for *The Morning Show.* As the rest of the team celebrated, I was at home, in the foetal position. For almost a week, I avoided my television and my BlackBerry—the two things I used the most. My senior producers were told I was at home with the flu. My only desire was to stay in the dark and away from people. Any people. Even my closest friend, Steven, struggled to make me talk. In the end, he convinced me to seek help.

In late June 2007, I was diagnosed with type II bipolar—a disorder characterised by sometimes debilitating mood swings. Psychiatrist Gordon Parker, considered one of Australia's leading experts on the condition, told me that people with bipolar often experience exhilarating highs where they feel they can do anything. Golfers see every blade of grass, and footballers, every play. It's a time of creativity and risk-taking, of impulsive shopping and sexual promiscuity. Everything he described sounded familiar. On the flipside, the depression can be crippling, and needs a lot more than counselling or psychotherapy to break. He told me that people with bipolar are at a greater risk of suicide—about a quarter try to end their lives.

As awful as all that sounded, I came away feeling slightly relieved. Being able to explain things would surely make them easier to beat. And if not, I figured my new regime of drugs would do the trick.

It was time to get back to work.

12

GETTING NEWS AND HAVING A NIGHTCAP

There's an old saying in television: you're only as good as your last ratings. And that meant I was doing fine in 2007, with *Sunrise, Weekend Sunrise* and *The Morning Show* all easily winning their slots.

Things weren't looking quite as good over at Channel Nine. New boss Jeffrey Browne knew he had to act fast to stop his network from faltering. A lawyer by trade, he was known by many as 'Buckets' because of his assertion that television stations were merely 'a bucket of contracts'. In mid-August, he was keen to throw one of those contracts at me.

He invited me to his apartment in Sydney's eastern suburbs. I didn't know what to expect but I was still keen to make an impression. 'I remember being at your house on the day you went to meet him,' says Rob McKnight. 'There you were ironing your shirt while the rest of us were watching television. We thought it was strange that you would ever iron a shirt, but you never told us who you were meeting until later.'

Browne told me that Nine's news machine was broken. It was certainly true that it could no longer claim to be number one; the combined efforts of *Sunrise*, *Today Tonight* and *Seven News* had made sure of that. He asked what I'd do if I were in charge.

I wasn't sure what he meant. In charge of a news bulletin, the *Today* show or something else? I ventured a ramble that pretty much covered the lot. I waxed lyrical about American trends, the need for newsreaders to become 'anchors' and the perils of following the leader. When I came up for air, he asked whether I'd like to run news and current affairs at Nine. The entire division. He told me I'd have his backing to 'smash the culture'. It was an extraordinary offer and, I knew, the opportunity of a lifetime. The only real problem: it wasn't at Channel Seven.

It was no secret that I coveted the job at Seven but always accepted I'd need to wait until Peter Meakin decided to retire. And given the loyalty shown to me by Seven's top brass, accepting Browne's offer was anything but straightforward. A few days passed before I texted him, seeking more time. His response hit home: 'As long as Meakin is there, they can't offer you what I'm offering you.'

I was fine with making editorial or spending decisions for my shows on the fly, but this was doing my head in. I called my closest friends together for a drink at a Sydney bar. Four of them worked at Seven; all five of them told me to accept the offer. I was starting to agree but wanted first to talk to Peter Meakin.

It was never my intention to play one network off against the other. I knew the job wasn't open at Seven, so accepted they couldn't match Nine's offer. I just felt that speaking to him was the right thing to do—he was my mentor as well as my boss. But, rather than offer advice, he picked up the phone. As I sat across from him in his office, Meakin called Channel Nine. He asked to be put through to Garry Linnell, who was still in the job Browne had offered to me. I watched in disbelief as he triggered a sequence of irreversible events.

'Garry, Peter Meakin here. Look, I'm sorry to be the one to tell you this but I thought you might like to know that Jeffrey Browne has offered your position to one of my people.'

I'd never seen anything like it. I wasn't sure whether to shout or cry. When he put down the phone, he turned to me with a grin; he always got immense satisfaction from causing mischief. He told me my future was at Seven, without acknowledging that he'd just stolen the choice from me. When I ask him about it now, he still feels he did nothing wrong. 'What else did you expect me to do? Was I meant to go "Oh, that's very nice. I'll just file that away"? It was an attempt to induce you to breach your contract. And, frankly, I thought I would crank it up for all it was worth.' And crank it up he did.

The episode became front-page news. 'Sources' at Nine claimed I'd never been offered the job and, while

I understood they'd been placed in an awkward position, I didn't like being called a liar. I leaked Browne's text messages to the press (a selfish act, to restore my ego).

Garry Linnell resigned on 23 August 2007. In a statement to the media, he said: 'It's become clear to me in recent weeks that I do not have the full support of the company. This has placed me in an untenable position.' It had. Browne, Meakin and I were all to blame.

***

Television executives like a drink. As legendary producer Gerald Stone once put it: 'Television runs on adrenalin and alcohol.' During his time at Channel Nine in the 1980s, it was an accepted ritual to end the day in the Third Floor Bar.

The place was an institution; producers and stars would drift up there for free booze and even freer thinking. Meakin was a regular. He tells me it's all a bit of a blur but does remember that some of Nine's biggest hits, like consumer program *Money*, were commissioned during late night drinks. 'Sometimes at eleven o'clock at night, we'd say, 'Yeah, that's a great idea,' and the show would be launched the following day.' No research, just instinct.

I've never known Meakin to be fond of research. I've sat through meetings where he's tuned out as findings are delivered with the researchers left to look at me with despair. As he puts it: 'I can't think of a single show that is successful because it's been the product of good research. I can think of many shows that researched well and then fell in a heap and others that researched badly but are giant successes. I think some of these research panels are just an invitation for participants to be self-congratulatory.' It's true that one dominant voice can skew the result. I've also seen people claim to watch SBS in an apparent attempt to look smarter but then prove unable to answer any questions about the channel.

The bar is long gone but the tradition continues. Sydney's Sofitel Wentworth Hotel is hardly the Channel Nine bar. But, while there's no pissing on walls, the guests do piss away money. Proudly five-star, the Wentworth remains the Liberal Party's preferred venue on election nights. It's also just a block from the *Sunrise* studio. We'd sometimes call in when we wanted to avoid the cheaper inner-city bars. They're often filled with bankers, who are even louder than television producers.

In January 2008, I joined a few TV mates for a Sofitel soiree; Paul Slater, now promoted to *Sunrise* director among them. 'It was one of those nights where you would just summon us to a bar and then spend the rest of the night shouting us all drinks without ever looking at the bill,' he says. A psychologist might label it a manic episode.

We talked shop and threw around ideas. The more vodka we drank, the better they seemed. We were in our own world, hardly noticing the lounge singer off to the side. That was, until he did something entirely unexpected at the Sofitel.

He wanted to know whether we'd seen his balls. His big, salty and brown balls. Just moments earlier, he'd been singing Sinatra; without a blink, this African-American with a voice straight out of New Orleans took on the persona of Chef from cult comedy *South Park.* He looked us straight in the eyes while urging us to suck on his chocolate salty balls.

I'm not sure what was funnier—his performance or the reaction to it. One woman kept looking at her husband in the hope he would explain what she was hearing. We gave the singer a standing ovation and I bought him a drink when he moseyed on over: 'Hey, fellas, I'm Beau.' He liked a laugh and a whiskey on ice. We immediately said he belonged on TV.

In the wake of my flirtation with Nine, Seven allowed me to design a new show, but not necessarily one for on air; rather, we'd make one episode—a pilot—just to see how it looked. To be honest, I knew this was only meant to appease me. These days, pilots are rarely green-lit for an on-air run. Most formats need to be proven in overseas markets before being rolled out in Australia. There are notable exceptions, including Seven's hugely successful *My Kitchen Rules.*

To me, late at night was where the action was; television's Holy Grail. In America, it's where you find some of the country's biggest stars, like David Letterman and Jimmy Fallon. It's a place for fun and surprises—watching it is the perfect way to go to bed with a smile. I'm also a firm believer that a strong late night show can help boost your breakfast show. It's a fairly basic theory: if Seven is the last channel you're watching before switching off the TV, then your TV will still be on Seven when you switch it back on the next morning.

In 2008, the commercial networks had little to offer in the slot, perhaps thinking of it is as simply too hard. It wasn't always like that. Graham Kennedy and Don Lane made their names late at night in the 1960s. Kennedy returned to the slot in the 1980s, alongside Ken Sutcliffe and then John Mangos, providing his unique, and often delightfully offensive, remarks about people in the news. He once observed that Queen Elizabeth didn't have bad breasts for someone her age.

In the 1990s, late night television was the domain of Steve Vizard and Clive Robertson. Vizard took a Letterman-style approach, with big studio audiences and interviews with big names, but it was Robertson who fascinated me. Ostensibly a newsreader, he'd often sit in the studio and sigh about the things he was reporting. If he didn't like how something was written, he'd point that out too, live on air, before looking off camera as if contemplating whether it was worth continuing.

In an interview with the ABC's Peter Thompson in 2005, he explained his approach to newsreading: 'If I thought a story was really important, I'd look at the camera and say, "This is a really important story," and the audience think, "Oh, this guy's a good filter". If you said, "Look, this is a silly item, I don't know why we're running it," and you run it and it *is* a silly item, you've got them. It's not a con.' It always struck me that Robertson had a powerful relationship with his viewers simply through being himself. This was a valuable lesson I would remember when putting together on-air teams.

I particularly liked his honesty about the way television news works. In the nineties, producers of the 6pm news lived in a bubble, deluding themselves that viewers didn't get news from anywhere else. If a story broke at 8pm, they'd report it the following day at 6pm, as if it had just happened. Robertson would point that out to his viewers with lines like: 'My show is often first with the news. If you don't believe me, watch how it's reported the following day.' His approach shows why so many network stars would love a crack at late night television, many feeling their real talents are constrained by overly produced primetime shows.

Deal or No Deal and *Weekend Sunrise* host Andrew O'Keefe was one such star. He'd been pushing for a late night show for years and I thought he deserved one. Trained as a lawyer and a natural at sketch comedy, he had the two things a host needs to walk and talk without help from producers: he was funny and smart. The network allowed him to pilot a late show in 2007, alongside his friend, the newsreader Simon Reeve. The show had potential but was never approved. I suspect it had something to do with the fact Andrew polarised viewers: they either loved him or hated him. To me, that mattered little because most people knew him only as a game show host. Perceptions can change quickly.

Hosts aren't the only ones who like the late night slot. Seven knew I was keen on entering the space. Rather than pointlessly make a pilot that would never be seen, I bypassed the programming department to form a new alliance.

A few months earlier, Channel Seven had launched an entirely new channel called 7HD. Seven's senior management, especially David Leckie, saw it as little more than a distraction, but knew it was necessary to meet new regulatory requirements. The federal government was on a crusade, quite rightly, to introduce digital television to Australia.

7HD's programming was hardly inspired—a mix of American shows that weren't good enough to air on Channel Seven or repeats of shows that we'd all rather forget. The man given oversight of 7HD, and the official title of general manager of program operations, was Tim McDonald, a non-threatening guy who everyone seemed to like, and who tended to operate in the shadows and away from the brutality of network politics. With 7HD anything but a priority, Tim was well placed simply to make sure it got on air without any fuss.

There was one other thing about Tim that I quite liked: he had an old-fashioned love of television. He started as a tape operator at Channel Ten in 1979, before working his way up the ladder and, unlike many television executives, actually knew how programs were made. He could tell you the difference between a jib and a dolly, and knew that gels weren't just for your skin. Perhaps he was a soft target, but it wasn't hard for me to convince him we had an opportunity to make history. I offered to create a brand-new show that would air on 7HD twice a week; it wouldn't cost much to make, so nobody could possibly object to it, but it would be the channel's first original production. That's the kind of stuff us TV geeks love. Tim was on board.

The NightCap would be a late night panel show that would cover news in an unconventional way. At the time, there was nothing similar on TV (Ten's highly successful *The Project* didn't start until a year later, in 2009). Our panel would consist mainly of journalists, but ones who could crack a joke or throw a grenade. All but one were people I'd worked with, so I knew what they could do without a straitjacket.

Paul Murray was a radio host with a very sharp tongue. His dishevelled look reminded me of American filmmaker Michael Moore, but he had views much further to the right. I'd always liked Paul, not just for his talent but also because he was the last to know he actually had any. For someone so confident on air, he had a surprising lack of confidence off air.

Jessica Rowe wears her heart on her sleeve. Famously 'boned' by Channel Nine as host of *Today,* she'd always had more to give than she'd been given the opportunity to offer. Unlike Paul, her views were more to the left. She'd argue passionately for the rights of asylum seekers and condemn any form of discrimination.

Monique Wright is super savvy and super smart. She'd been a reporter on *Sunrise* for years and never showed any inhibitions. She'd speak freely about anything from relationships to the weather, making her invaluable on a panel.

Matt White is one of the slickest presenters on television. From major sports events to tabloid TV shows, Matt has done it all. He's cool under pressure and can keep things moving. His role would be to steer the conversation.

The final member of the panel was the only one who was untried. Zach Douglas had been propelled to fame after almost winning *Big Brother,* and was what the media likes to call 'flamboyant'. Street smart but still naive, he struck me as someone who could bring a touch of attitude and unpredictability. Others on my production team weren't as convinced. Rob McKnight was the show's supervising producer, and when I asked him recently about Zach, he offered this frank appraisal: 'Sometimes you let your groin get in the way of your decisions. Zach was a groin decision.' Paul Slater, who would direct the show, agrees. 'That wasn't your brain hiring him.' In my defence, Zach was popular with younger demographics; *The NightCap* would be aimed at a different crowd than Seven's traditional audience, and I felt he could help get us traction.

And that brings us back to our American crooner, Beau. When we saw him at the Sofitel, we knew he had to be part of the show—if for no other reason than his deep and ballsy laugh. He didn't take much convincing: 'Sure, boys, just bring the whiskey.'

The NightCap was a very cheap show to make—I've had lunches that cost more. It would be produced entirely by *Sunrise* staff, for free. The presenters would be paid a small amount per show and Beau's glass would always be full. We did it because making television was what we did. It made us happy. Well, usually. As with the launch of *The Morning Show*, my mind was again caught in a spiral on the eve of *The NightCap*' s debut.

Rob McKnight saw it first-hand. 'You were barely acknowledging us,' he says now. 'I think it was a great indicator of what you were doing to yourself.

You still had *Sunrise,* you still had *The Morning Show* and now you were working late at night as well.' I always know when the black dog bites; I'm never in denial. I try to fend it off, but often end up lost in my own world. I can sense people around me, but find it hard to engage. I just want to crawl away. Given I had a similar episode while launching *The Morning Show,* you could perhaps put this one down to stress, but I didn't. I'd endured many stressful episodes at *Sunrise,* but few of them brought on depression.

There is no doubt a lack of sleep didn't help, as it has a proven link to depression, but there was something else. I've tried to track some of the more dire episodes through my life and they all tended to coincide with moments of major transition, such as changing schools or launching a new TV show, like *The NightCap.* It was a double-edged sword because I was often on a high when planning a new show but, just as I reached the top of the mountain, I sometimes fell down the cliff. Still, in my business, the show really must go on, it's not just a saying. During my time at Seven, I always had colleagues who not only protected me but picked up the slack.

An hour before our first show, Paul Murray and I went to Hungry Jack's. The other hosts were in makeup but, being the loveable teddy, Paul tended to come as he was. We walked up Martin Place, our Whoppers in hand, and joked about the glamour of TV. He asked for any last-minute advice—I told him what I tell every presenter: don't overthink. (I think he still did for the first few episodes. At one point, his friend and director Paul Slater urged him to pull things back, knowing he'd been making me nervous.)

Paul Murray's wouldn't be the first face to appear on *The NightCap.* That honour went to Beau. Television shows considered a tad risqué always began with a warning—just so nobody complained when kids saw something they shouldn't. (That said, viewers always complain. About anything and everything. It's weird when they don't.) We wanted our classification announcement to stand out from the crowd.

At 10.30pm on Tuesday, 12 February 2008, Beau, with his big smiling face, walked in front of the camera and put everyone on notice:

Well, hey, guys, it's Beau here.

The NightCap is classified M.

You never know what these crazy folks might say.

It might contain some coarse language, adult themes and sexual references.

We recommend viewing by a mature audience.

And then there was his trademark laugh, which we allowed to run its natural course of about six seconds. *The NightCap* was on the air.

Now, at this point, it's perhaps worth pointing out that we had no idea of how many people were watching, as ratings for 7HD were never collected. We could have had a thousand viewers or we could have a million viewers. Actually, who are we kidding? We would have had a few thousand at most.

That meant we had to broaden our scope, so we billed *The NightCap* as the most interactive show on television. Apart from broadcasting on 7HD, we streamed the show live. This is common now, but was a novelty back then. We took talkback calls and read out emails as they came in (Twitter was relatively new), and we set up webcams around the studio, so you could watch us from multiple angles.

Our first story set the tone, as Matt White made it clear we had a different style from Seven's 6pm news.

Matt: Well, how's this for a declaration?

America's top military man reckons al-Qaeda has now been forced out of Iraq.

So how does he explain the latest round of suicide attacks?

Here comes your reality check.

Different style and different content. Foreign stories were rarely a priority for commercial news services, which went nuts for local crime and the cost of petrol, but left the other stuff to the ABC. We felt our late night audience craved something more and could handle a broader conversation. That's not to suggest we were exclusively highbrow—far from it. The show is probably best remembered (if at all) for our revelations about men in bed.

After the first few shows, it was obvious to us that Zach's contribution was limited. He could talk about fashion and gossip, but little else, and would just stare off camera during debates on politics or world affairs. Our attempt to give him a bigger role blew up in our face. Actually, that's probably a poor choice of words, given what happened.

Our new segment, 'Ask Zach', allowed viewers to submit personal problems for Zach's honest feedback. The first email came from Lisa of Melbourne: *My boyfriend won't kiss me when we're having sex. Why do you think that is and what can I do?*

Zach got straight to the point. 'Don't give him head beforehand. Men don't like the idea that they're tasting themselves.'

Silence from the panel—so Zach offered more.

'It's quite known in gay sex, y'know, like, well, that's a gay man's dream. You get in, you get out, there's no ... y'know what I mean?'

I'm not sure Jess did. Paul Murray was nodding with a wry smile, urging Zach to continue. Matt tried to get things back on track, by calling on Monique: 'I think it's just an intimacy-level thing. A woman is a lot more affectionate than a man,' she offered.

There, all better. Surely. And, besides, nobody was watching anyway, right?

Wrong.

The following day, the tabloids reported it with the usual level of disdain, calling the segment 'sordid' and 'tacky'. It probably was, but was that such a bad thing? We'd promised an edgier show.

We had a bigger problem than the papers, though. David Leckie's wife, Skye, was apparently watching as well. She didn't offer a rave review to David, who, by that time, was tucked up in bed. Rob McKnight sums up the team's feeling: 'Shockingly, a television show aimed at a younger audience didn't appeal to an older woman.'

A week later, I moved Zach back to his home city of Melbourne and made him *The NightCap'* s gossip contributor. Instead of sitting around the panel for the full half-hour, he was now back in his comfort zone. We crossed to him only once a show, for a glimpse into a world he knew only too well. The papers, of course, said he'd been demoted, because of his 'sordid' insights on sex. He really wasn't—I simply felt sorry for him, and wanted to save him any further embarrassment from having to talk about things that didn't interest him.

Still, by now, David Leckie had had enough. First his wife had been at him and now the papers kept talking about a show he hadn't even seen. After just ten episodes, he swung the axe. Both Tim McDonald and I urged him to reconsider, but he very rarely does.

7HD may not have had many viewers, but it was a valuable place to experiment. Producers could road-test new shows and try out emerging talent without risking having a high-profile failure. You'd only switch something to the main channel once it had been shown to work Off-Broadway.

To me, it was a missed opportunity. *The NightCap* was just finding its feet: Beau had developed a cult following, and the panel was thriving, as, with Zach's removal, its chemistry hit the mark; the feedback was good and the show was fun. It was even making me laugh as my depression faded away. Producers will often cry foul at decisions made from above but, in this case, I think many would agree that Leckie got it wrong. Still, *The NightCap'* s premature axing didn't sway me from pursuing a late-night vehicle. A year later, I met the boss of Sydney's Star Casino, Sid Vaikunta. He was planning the casino's redevelopment and I was keen for him to factor in a television studio for a live, late night show. The pitch called for Star to pick up all costs in exchange for us broadcasting from there each night; their big money for our big profile. A casino was the one place you'd be guaranteed a studio audience each night, as the pokies crowd never sleeps. Star also had an unrivalled view of Sydney's skyline, which could have served as the perfect set.

No one could accuse Sid of lacking ambition. He'd cut his teeth amid the bright lights of Atlantic City, where he ran marketing divisions at some of its biggest casinos. The Sydney gig would be the first where he called all the shots. Sid liked my idea and revealed he had plans of his own to bring some of his high-profile friends, like Elton John, down under. We mused that he, and other performers of his ilk, could perform at the Star before appearing on the television show, just needing to walk from one room to the other. It seemed like the perfect marriage.

Sadly, though, marriage was proving a difficult ideal for Sid. He was sacked just a few months later, when two women accused him of sexual harassment, with one claiming the casino boss had groped her in the back of a limousine. He and his wife then left for Dubai.

I thought about trying again, with his replacement, but decided to face reality.

Television often comes down to luck and timing—both of them had denied me a lengthy late night plunge. I was starting to think I'd never escape the snap, crackle and pop of breakfast television.

13

A STAR IS TORN

'Justin who?'

Sunrise entertainment producer Michael Turtle couldn't believe I was asking this question. 'Bieber,' he replied, 'and he's the hottest teen star on the planet! Apparently.'

Turtle conceded he didn't know much about him either, but his contact at Universal Music assured him the kid was hot. It was March 2010 and Bieber had just released his debut album. Universal was bringing the then sixteen year old to Australia and wanted him to perform on the show. I wasn't convinced he was *Sunrise* material: few in the office had heard of him and teenage girls weren't exactly our market.

Justin Bieber grew up in the Canadian city of Stratford, with an unwavering passion for music. He taught himself how to play the drums, piano, guitar and trumpet, all by the age of twelve. His proud mum would rave about him to family, before posting videos of him on YouTube so they could see him perform. Those videos didn't just impress the rellies. Girls he didn't know stumbled on to them too and started sharing them en masse. Here was social media at work—Bieber didn't need a music company to promote him, YouTube was spreading the word. Girls were obsessed; not just with his talent, but with his floppy hair. By mid-2007, Bieber's clips had been viewed more times than those of any other singer in Canada. His mum described his success as the work of God and even went on a religious television show to express her thanks. God wasn't done yet, though.

Later that year, someone else clicked on a Bieber video entirely by mistake. Scooter Braun was an American music hotshot renowned for turning singers into brands. Having seen the video, he wanted in on the Bieber craze and reached out to his mum. She was cautious but, after consulting her church, she agreed to deal with the fast-talking New Yorker. A week later, Justin Bieber was singing for one of his idols: the music star Usher. Braun and Usher had just started a production company and Bieber would be their first signing. The innocent then thirteen year old from Stratford had hit the big time and was about to meet the world.

We still doubted his appeal in Australia but his backstory was enough for us to book him, albeit for just a short interview and a quick performance. 'He's bigger than you think he is,' insisted Martha Pavlakis from Universal Music. She wanted us to stage a major *Sunrise* concert for him—something we reserved for only the biggest acts. 'You need to trust me,' she continued, 'he's already had 150 million views on YouTube.' It was not a bad argument. Young girls might not have been regular *Sunrise* viewers, but who were we to stand in the way of high ratings? We'd take viewers however they came. Bieber would get his concert.

Sunrise does music television better than any other show in Australia. I still believe that, long after they've stopped paying my wage. The team knows how to make things look good. During my decade with the show, we hosted everyone from Pink to Keith Urban, and those concerts didn't come cheap: each cost at least $80000. There's money required for staging, big screens, satellite trucks and even portaloos. *Sunrise* would cover the entire bill; the music companies had big names but very little money. Our only demand was exclusivity.

When that wasn't met, I'd make them pay a much bigger price. In 2008, *Today'* s Richard Wilkins secured an interview with Kylie Minogue, thanks mainly to their longstanding relationship. Having spent decades reporting entertainment, Wilkins was well connected. Despite this fact, I was enraged by his exclusive—it was simple competition but I took it personally. My anger was directed at Minogue's music company, Warner.

For almost two months, *Sunrise* stopped taking Warner's calls. It was a hardline approach that sent a shiver down the spines of Warner's competitors. The rules were now clear: big interviews and performances were to be offered to us first, leaving *Today* with our scraps. It was grossly unreasonable, but most toed the line out of fear of being locked out by the market leader. Given our relationship with Universal Music, we were willing to risk $80000 on someone we knew little about. We still needed to minimise the risk, so publicist Penny Heath and social media manager Luke Buckle were given the challenge of ensuring every single Bieber fan knew he'd be performing on *Sunrise.*

Penny and Luke were taken aback by how easy that was. Justin's 'Beliebers' were a well-organised army, with the most advanced communications system known to man. The *Sunrise* Twitter account suddenly had thousands of new followers—and then thousands more. A few quick tweets from us were instantly retweeted. We'd never seen anything like it and we were still ten days out from the concert.

The tweets swung his fans into action. The following morning, we got clues there would be an invasion, when girls started lurking outside our building. They were on a reconnaissance mission but we weren't sure why; there was nothing for them to see. They carried posters and wore shirts, all emblazoned with Justin's baby face and floppy hair. Channel Seven staffers were accosted as they turned up for work: 'When's Justin coming?' 'Can we meet him?' 'Can you tell Justin I love him?' I remember Peter Meakin walking up the stairs, grumpily asking, 'Who the fuck is Justin?'

We weren't the only ones being harassed. Kids hounded their parents with desperate pleas to get them to the concert. Some were booking flights from interstate to be there on the morning. Even old friends of mine just happened to use that time to reconnect: 'Oh, Adam, how have you been? Been meaning to catch up for ages. You well? Oh, while I think of it, I notice you have Justin Bieber performing. Any chance you could arrange for little Sally to meet him?'

All this for just three songs. We were starting to accept that Martha Pavlakis was right: Justin Bieber really was bigger than we thought.

***

When Seven moved to central Sydney in August 2004, it was, of course, considered a significant coup for *Sunrise.* Rather than being stuck within the artificial confines of sets, we'd now be surrounded by the action of a pulsing CBD. In our minds, we'd only add to that energy by broadcasting live events from Martin Place, our own slimmed-down version of New York's Rockefeller Center.

We failed to factor in a group of pretentious party poopers who occupied a building close by. From the time we'd moved in, the old-school lawyers had been agitating against us. They wanted us to keep everything inside and pretend Martin Place never existed. Their gripe was over excessive noise. They felt that any fun outside would disturb their serious work inside. We did manage to stage a few small concerts just outside our studio, with acts like Ben

Lee. Each time we did, the lawyers would huff and puff all the way to Town Hall.

We weren't willing to surrender without a fight, so took one of our own lawyers to the council. Rebecca Barnett is commercially savvy and tends to win arguments using simple common sense. She joined Channel Seven executive David Porter and me for a meeting with the council's decision makers. This wasn't just about the Bieber concert. We wanted them to understand the benefits of having a television station in the heart of their city, and needed an easy way to stage outside events without ongoing disputes.

I found it hard to keep my cool as the bureaucrats told us we were merely one of many who wanted to use Martin Place. Barnett reminded them that Seven was now a rather significant city tenant. David Porter pointed out that our concerts would air just after 7am and be over before the business day even began. In the end, the council agreed to consider each event on a case-by-case basis. It was a cop-out that was meant to appease the lawyers while pretending they were doing us a favour. In this instance, they told us, Martin Place wasn't available for Bieber and his army.

Finding a suitable venue for a breakfast television concert isn't easy. You need somewhere that doesn't just have space but a backdrop that wows a national audience. The Opera House is always the most obvious choice. The front steps have hosted everything from

Crowded House's farewell concert to the final of *Australian Idol,* but its neighbours also intervened to stop Bieber. It wasn't lawyers this time, but millionaire residents who'd monopolised a prized slice of the harbour. A 7am wake-up call was apparently too much for them to bear.

We eventually settled on an area on the opposite side of Circular Quay. The forecourt of the cruise ship terminal ticked all of our boxes: plenty of space for the crowd and our trucks, Sydney's iconic skyline as our set and no whining neighbours. Two days before the concert, I did a site inspection with Scooter Braun. He reminded me of a melodramatic bride on the day before her wedding. 'I want the stage there,' he proclaimed. 'This area roped off. Justin will enter from here.' I don't think he made eye contact with us once. My production manager, Dave Masala, let slip a smile, pre-empting a clash he now knew was inevitable. 'So, you have all that?' Braun asked in his patronising way.

'Sure, and none of that will be happening,' I offered in return.

I then let loose with my own rant, about how *Sunrise* was picking up the bill, so we'd decide where the stage went and which areas would be roped off. Braun's posse looked at me as if I were arguing with the Lord. 'Fine,' he conceded, 'but you're going to need more crowd barriers.' As would soon be revealed, he was absolutely right. We went in grossly unprepared.

The concert was set for Monday morning, 26 April. As Dave was overseeing the stage construction on Sunday afternoon, he called me with an uncharacteristic note of concern in his voice. Dozens of young girls, some aged just ten, were already there and planned to camp out overnight. They'd come equipped with sleeping bags and energy drinks but without much supervision. Dave could only spot one lone mum sitting in the distance. We brought in a security guard to serve as a replacement guardian and asked local police to increase patrols.

By two-thirty on Monday morning, we knew we'd need a lot more support. Car after car was pulling up, all full of girls quite clearly on a mission. They'd slam the door and run straight for the stage. Again, very few parents bothered to stick around. An hour later, thousands of girls were now fighting for position, even though there was all the space in the world. They surged forward, leading to an agonising crush up front. Things were turning dangerous and our pleas for calm proved useless. Extra police were now on the scene and doing what they could to pull the crowd back. They were hampered by the fact that our main technical crew weren't yet at work, meaning we couldn't use the public address system. I jumped on stage to urge some common sense but my own voice was nothing against the squealing of the horde.

Ten days earlier, social media was our friend as it helped spread word about the concert. Now it was our enemy, when a single tweet caused hysteria. Rumour reached a sea of glinting phones that Justin Bieber was on his way. It was only 3.30am, almost three hours before Bieber would even wake up. The tweet caused a stampede and not just at the venue. Police reported girls running through Sydney streets, with a reckless disregard for their safety. We issued our own tweet saying the rumour was false, but the girls seemed unconvinced.

A police sergeant pleaded with me to switch the stage lights on, so we could get a better sense of who in the crowd needed help. That quickly backfired, as the girls took it to mean the concert was about to start. As they started jumping and throwing their arms around, some of the smaller girls were being hurt and there was little we could do.

We finally got the public address system to work and declared the concert would be cancelled unless everyone took five steps back. Again, it made no difference. Those at the front were being crushed against the barriers. It was awful to watch. Police managed to lift almost 100 to safety, only to have them burst out crying about losing their places. Others were now begging for water and a *Sunrise* producer ran to a nearby convenience store to buy every bottle they had. We were scrambling to recover a situation that was now out of control. By 4.30am, at least 5000 teens and tweens had shown up, and many of them were hyperventilating.

A police inspector joined me on a balcony at the nearby cruise terminal to discuss what should happen. As we looked down at the crush, she said she wanted the concert to be cancelled, arguing that serious injuries were possible. She was also worried that, as the crowd kept growing, some girls might fall into Sydney Harbour. It was still dark, meaning rescues would prove difficult. The inspector was undoubtedly right but, rather than insisting we call the concert off, she allowed us to try one last thing.

Two large screens book-ended the stage and we used them to issue an ultimatum. In big black letters, we made it clear that: JUSTIN BIEBER WILL NOT COME UNLESS EVERYONE TAKES FIVE STEPS BACK. Instead of complying, they simply screamed. It was a synchronised tantrum that seemed impossible to stop. Just before 5am, police ran out of patience, ordering the concert be cancelled.

The stage announcer kept shouting: 'Go home, there will be no concert. Go home. It's cancelled.' Most thought we were bluffing, until police moved in to force them away. As reality set in, the girls became inconsolable. Many collapsed on their knees, with the kind of despair you'd see during a day of orchestrated mourning in North Korea.

I couldn't hang about to pick up the pieces. The plan for our entire show had just been ditched, with only an hour before we went to air. On the way back to the studio, the solution became obvious.

Breakfast radio was going nuts over the hysteria at *Sunrise.* Even New South Wales deputy police commissioner Dave Owens joined the fray, with an interview on 2GB. 'I would question why there weren't a larger number of parents down there,' he complained. 'We had twelve-, thirteen-, fourteen-year-old girls at 3am and 4am. We asked them numerous times once the crush started to occur for our directions to be obeyed for the safety of these kids, but they would not abide by our directions. They left us with no option but to cancel the concert.'

Everyone was talking about us, so we should as well. We'd make ourselves the morning's top story, with our inside account of what went wrong. And, just like the deputy commissioner, we'd throw the spotlight on parents to, if for no other reason, overshadow our own obvious failure to be better prepared.

Once again, we failed to factor in the power of Twitter and its ability to amplify rumour into fact. Shortly after going on air, new tweets emerged that Bieber would be appearing in our studio at Martin Place. We had no such plan but that hardly mattered. As 2GB put it, 'a riot' was now underway in central Sydney.

Teenage girls were again running through city streets but, this time, there were many more cars to contend with. The increased danger failed to slow them, with few bothering even to check for traffic. Hovering choppers captured the mayhem, allowing us to broadcast it live. Police set up roadblocks for safe passage, knowing it would be useless to talk sense into the girls. The riot squad then scrambled to Martin Place and formed a human wall around our studio. They couldn't turn the girls away but they could at least try to stop them from being smothered against the glass.

Within thirty minutes, Martin Place became a mosh pit. Police weren't happy and I'm sure the lawyers next door weren't either. I, on the other hand, was over the moon. The turmoil at *Sunrise* was now being reported across all media. Even Channel Nine was covering it live but the best place to watch it was obviously *Sunrise.* I knew our ratings would be through the roof. Such is the often shallow and selfish thinking of those who make television.

Social media again fuelled the fire as Bieber himself took to Twitter. 'I love my fans,' he wrote, 'I love it here in Australia ... and I want to sing.' He followed that up by absolving himself of any responsibility. 'I WANT TO MAKE THIS CLEAR ... I DONT CANCEL ... I WOKE UP THIS MORNING TO THE POLICE CANCELING THE SHOW FOR SAFETY REASONS.' When Justin speaks, his army listens. The hashtag #LetJustinSing became the most popular trending topic that morning not just in Australia but the world. There were five Bieber-related tweets per second.

The chant outside followed suit. 'Let Bieber sing!' was all we could hear, as if we'd muzzled their idol. You know things are tense when even the riot squad looks worried. We had to find a way to appease the masses.

With unabated chaos outside, senior police met with us inside my office and offered an unexpected solution: give the girls what they want. They felt if Bieber came to the studio for a quick appearance, the crowd would finally head home.

Despite the 'don't blame us' tweets from the Bieber camp, they turned out to be the most difficult to convince of this approach. 'Universal and his management were worried the whole thing was too much of a mess,' remembers entertainment producer Michael Turtle. 'I was on the phone for much of the morning with Martha Pavlakis, trying to convince them to come. In the end, they came but would only agree to do one song and no interview. He just wanted to read out a short statement apologising for the fiasco but blaming it on *Sunrise.*' Bless him.

Nobody at *Sunrise* is entirely sure how we got Bieber into the building. Folklore has it that he was put in a box for the drive into our loading dock. He was certainly small enough to fit in it. Once he reached the studio, our floor manager, Nic Connell, gently ushered him into position. Bieber then snapped, 'Don't ever fucking touch me again.' We'd had some of the world's biggest stars in that studio but never with that type of lip. A sound technician from the Bieber team urged Nic not to take offence because 'he tells us that all the time'.

Bieber's performance ensured collective rapture outside the glass. The girls were screaming so loudly that nobody would have heard a note. Television pictures showed members of the riot squad covering their ears. Sections of the crowd soon broke free, to make a run for Channel Seven's front door. They spilled on to busy Elizabeth Street, which then had to be closed. Peak-hour buses were soon queuing for miles. Our security staff and the police were ferociously yelling at everyone to move back from the door.

Inside, Bieber had finished his song. Despite the silly agreement that he would only read a prepared statement, David Koch and Melissa Doyle hit him up with some questions. 'I was really looking forward to getting out there (to perform for the fans),' Bieber told them. 'It gets crazy sometimes.' He then confirmed he was single and that he was looking for a girl 'with nice eyes, nice smile, someone who makes me laugh' You can imagine what that did to the crowd outside. One girl even broke her knee while trying to grab his attention.

Kochie asked Bieber about the role Usher had played in his life. 'Usher has given me some great advice,' he replied, 'like staying humble. I have some great family members, such great friends who make sure I don't get arrogant.' Nic Connell was heard to scoff off set.

Bieber then agreed to one final request. He joined our weather presenter, Grant Denyer, to walk up to the studio window. He faced the crowd and formed a love heart with his hands.

I reckon that was the scariest moment of the morning. You could hear the noise from the other side of the city; it caused some Channel Seven staff actually to move back from the windows. As police held on tight, Bieber gave his instructions. 'I would love to stay and hang,' he told his fans, 'but you have to go. The police say you've got to go.'

Eventually, they did. Eight went by ambulance. Twelve others were treated outside the studio after fainting.

We sat through a series of debriefs with senior police and council officials about what went wrong and how to avoid a repeat. We made all the right noises and feigned concern but, from our point of view, it was a near-perfect show. Ratings were up by almost 20 per cent that morning and we were again the talk of the town. Music historians said Australia had seen nothing like it since Beatlemania in 1964.

A few days after the frenzy, David Koch put us back in the Bieber limelight while being interviewed by a Sydney radio station. Kochie shared Nic Connell's encounter with the listeners and then offered Bieber's minders some advice: 'I thought maybe someone should drag him aside and give him a bit of a slap.'

The Bieber army turned on Koch, led by their commander himself. 'I was raised to respect others and not gossip ... nor gossip with anger,' Bieber posted on Twitter. 'I know my friends, family and fans know the person I am. Hearing adults spread lies and rumors is part of the job I guess.' The Bieber camp insisted that if someone did swear, it wouldn't have been sweet little Justin, but maybe his manager, Scooter Braun. I guess they figured everyone would believe that. For the record, other *Sunrise* staffers also heard Bieber's outburst.

The Bieber saga was a fast-moving lesson in the fanaticism of young girls, the power of social media and the carefully managed spin of pop stars. On his way out of Australia, Justin Bieber offered one last tweet, which did state a fact: 'Thanks everyone ... it's been an amazing experience.'

***

As is evident from the Bieber brouhaha, of the almost 5000 people interviewed by *Sunrise* each year, big-name stars are usually the ones viewers remember. As can also be seen from the Bieber brouhaha, they're often the ones producers remember too but not always for the same reasons.

Michael Richards will always be better known as Cosmo Kramer from the hit US sitcom *Seinfeld.* He travelled to Australia in October 2004, to promote the release of the series on DVD, and *Sunrise* was one of his first stops. When he turned up on set in his dressing gown, we figured we were in for a treat. We even allocated the segment extra time, knowing that once the jokes started rolling, we wouldn't want them to end.

How wrong we were.

Richards was every bit as awkward as Kramer but not in the way we expected. The dressing gown would be as funny as things got; every question was met with responses of just a few words. We weren't sure if he was rude or just shy. Kochie tried one last thing, asking, rather crassly, whether Richards was 'free balling' under his dressing gown. The actor offered a three-second chuckle under his breath before looking off set.

It was cringe-worthy television and we couldn't wait for it to end.

The encounter changed the way *Sunrise* conducted interviews with comedians. From that point on, they were asked whether they'd prefer to see our questions in advance—something we'd never offer any other guest. Rather than having segments fall flat on air, we urged them to prepare answers in the same way they'd write material for stand-up. Perhaps that's not the most ethical approach, but making television that rates is no laughing matter.

***

Comedians aren't the only celebrities who can make for awkward television. In 2005, Heath Ledger spent an entire interview with our entertainment reporter, Katherine Tulich, peeling an orange. He seemed engrossed in it: no matter what Katherine did, she couldn't get the actor's attention.

To be fair to Ledger, his interview with Katherine was only one of many he had to do that day to promote his new film, *Lords of Dogtown.* While doing publicity, actors are often expected to maintain their enthusiasm from sunrise until sunset, no matter how many times they get asked the same questions. It's painful for them but, in this case, it was painful for our viewers as well.

Kochie and Mel later read out emails from viewers who felt fame had gone to Ledger's head. His family, watching from Perth, told him about the backlash. To his enormous credit, he then sent a personal letter to Katherine.

> I would like to apologise for my lack of enthusiasm to answer questions in the interview. It was one of about 60 interviews I completed in that sitting and it sounds like you landed the dud. I remember peeling that orange and eating it through the interview. In hindsight, it probably wasn't a polite thing to do. I was just hungry and a little dehydrated.

It wasn't often you'd get an apology like that from a star. The then twenty-six year old also told Katherine that he was still figuring out how to play the game.

***

She might now be one of the world's biggest stars, but in 2008, people were just discovering the irrepressible talent of Lady Gaga. Unfortunately, they weren't seeing much of that talent when she appeared on *Sunrise* in what was her first live television performance.

We'd booked her to perform at a special outside broadcast from Melbourne's Federation Square leading up to the AFL Grand Final. As she walked on stage, in a skin-toned body stocking, the crowd of footy supporters watched on, bemused. She then performed what would become her chart-topping single 'Just Dance'. But nobody did. Most were only waiting around to hear Mike Brady sing 'Up There Cazaly'. Those at home weren't dancing either. They'd noticed what we'd noticed: Lady Gaga didn't appear to actually be singing. As one blogger wrote on Brisbane's *Courier Mail* website, 'That was the worst "live" performance I have ever seen.'

Given the value *Sunrise* placed on live music, we considered that a significant problem. Music companies knew that we'd never allow performers to mime on the show; it would undermine their credibility and ours. I yelled at my entertainment producer, Rachel

Lees. 'That was undoubtedly one of the most difficult days of my career,' she later told me. 'I protested but you had already decided Gaga was lip-syncing and were livid. I was mid-sentence when you hung up on me.' She's right. I wasn't buying it and told Kochie and Mel to apologise on air.

That upped the stakes for Lady Gaga, who issued a statement of her own: 'I was sick the day of the show but I absolutely, 100 per cent, was singing live. I have never lip-synced and I never will.' Rachel agrees, 'I was on the ground, and I maintain she was singing. I heard her.'

Gaga had picked up a Melbourne lurgy and was worried about her voice. Before walking on stage, she told the sound engineer to pump up the pre-recorded backing track and pull down the volume of her microphone. So, yes, she'd been singing but very few people heard it.

Lady Gaga never forgave my aspersions—she once said she couldn't believe a queen could do such a thing. It was no accident that she never went back to *Sunrise* until I was no longer there.

***

Seven's own stars weren't always angels either and it was wardrobe that caused the most angst. Hosts rarely fork out their own money for clothes they wear on air; network stylists use deals with designers and department stores to keep them looking sharp. It's simple enough for the men—Kochie and Beretts turn up for work each day to find a pressed shirt and two or three ties from which to choose (for many years, the pair went without ties completely, making the job even easier). Many female presenters, though, believe that stylists play favourites, with better clothes and better jewellery always allocated to someone else.

The tension between Chris Bath and then *Weekend Sunrise* presenter Samantha Armytage was legendary. Sam was never afraid to take digs at Chris and even dubbed her 'Bath Vader'. Chris then arrived at work one day with a light sabre. Things got even sillier when they had to appear together in a network promo but turned up wearing similar shirts. The producer had to ask a news director to intervene before Sam would agree to change her outfit.

I should confess to my own petty feud with Chris. Despite us being close when I joined Channel Seven, we didn't speak for almost four years; we wouldn't even acknowledge each other when sharing a lift. The ice wasn't broken until we worked together on the current affairs show *Sunday Night.* Remarkably, neither of us could remember what started the saga—it had simply gone on for so long that we felt we'd passed the point of no return.

Those who have television's biggest egos and are capable of throwing the biggest tantrums are not the stars, but those who produce their shows and run the networks. But, as I was about to learn, it's never too late to change your ways.

14

FAREWELL, SUNRISE

Sunrise Executive Producer Adam Boland has cut back on his 24/7 TV obsession, finding a life outside work after falling head over heels in love with a man working in an unrelated industry.

His new partner—a Sydney architect named Julian—is credited with showing workaholic Boland 'greater intellectual' pursuits outside of television.

Producers are meant to stay behind the camera, not in front of it; the stars are the ones who make news, not their anonymous masters. The *Daily Telegraph* story about my love life, though, was only one of many. My critics argued I brought those articles on myself, by big-noting at every opportunity. Some even accused me of trying to claim full credit for the success of *Sunrise.* But I knew it was always a team effort.

There's no doubt that in my earlier years at Seven, I enjoyed the attention I got. It was good for my ego and I felt it was good for *Sunrise.* The show's meteoric rise had placed a spotlight on the small team behind it and, in particular, me, as the young EP. Journalists would write about my Converse sneakers and so-called baby face while labelling me a wunderkind of television. It was a tag we joked about in the office. Also, as time went by, I'd publicly defend the show whenever it was attacked. From the Sunlies affair to the fallout from Bieber, I'd put my head up as the one to be kicked. Some saw that as me seeking attention. I saw it as me doing my job.

Come 2010, I'd been talked about so often that my private life felt as if it had become public. I'm not sure anyone outside of media circles would have been all that interested, but the articles just kept on coming. I suspect my sexuality also played a role in capturing the attention of gossip writers.

> Boland came out three years ago after ending a relationship with *Sunrise* producer Yoko Shimizu and then he hooked up with another producer from the show, Michael Pell.

The *Daily Telegraph* even had sources willing to spill the beans.

> 'Julian appears in his late 20s and seems a really nice guy and it's genuine to say Adam is happy and has a whole new perspective on life,' another source said.

At least the source was right. For the first time in my life, there seemed to be something more important than television. Julian Wong's influence on me was immense. He'd never watched breakfast TV, nor heard of Kochie and Mel. He was interested in reading and learning about the world. Julian also loved meeting people and was always fascinated to hear new stories. I'd take him to parties where he wouldn't hesitate to walk up to celebrities. It was fun watching their often-bemused reactions when he asked, with genuine curiosity, what they did for work. He meant no offence; he simply didn't know who they were.

Julian grew up mainly in Australia but his parents later moved back to Hong Kong. It was a city I'd been to mostly for work and it never struck me as somewhere I'd make a priority to return. When I did go back, with Julian in April 2010, he introduced me to an entirely new place. For a few weeks, we lived like locals. We'd walk the busy streets of Kowloon, venture to New Territories and get caught in a storm while eating fish on Lamma Island. All of a sudden, Australia felt so small. Unlike other times I'd been overseas, now I had no desire to return home. I stopped checking my phone and lost interest in the shows I was producing. I'd become immersed in a different way of life and it was one that got me thinking about my future.

Back in Australia, it was becoming increasingly obvious that Peter Meakin's position would never be mine. Leaks kept appearing in the papers that Seven's director of news in Brisbane, Rob Raschke, was the favourite for the job. A few years earlier, that would have shaken me to the core. I'd been denied the Nine gig with hopes of better things at Seven. Now, though, I felt differently. I was disappointed but not devastated. I felt it could even be a blessing in disguise.

Work had become more of a chore than fun. I'd grown despondent due to the daily news cycle. Climate change deniers were dominant and asylum seekers were demonised. There was a time I'd have used *Sunrise* to try to make a difference but, suddenly, I just felt disconnected from our viewers. I was also starting to think I'd played all my cards in breakfast television, and so was becoming a liability to the show. A good executive producer needs passion and mine was beginning to fade.

That all came as news to Peter Meakin.

Meetings in Meakin's office tend to be fairly brief. Those who work for him see him more as a wise old owl than as a micromanager. He'll make you feel better about your decisions, or challenge you to reconsider them, but rarely gets bogged down in detail. Once he imparts his wisdom, he usually looks away. That's the cue to get up and leave.

I was at one such meeting in June 2010 but as he gave me the cue, I gave him some news: I'd decided to leave Channel Seven. Julian and I had plans to move to Hong Kong. We'd even made an offer on a rundown flat in Mongkok. I had no idea what I'd do there, but that was part of the attraction. Julian knew he could get work as an architect and we had enough money in the bank to get by.

News of my decision was soon reported in the press. In an interview with the *Daily Telegraph*, Meakin seemed in denial, telling them, 'He's not going anywhere else and we do have an option to keep him on.' He'd clearly boned up on my contract by the time he spoke to the *Australian*: 'Adam has talked to me and we hope to change his mind.' Meakin's unwavering belief in me was, and remains, greatly humbling. Despite campaigning for his job in 2007, I knew he'd be one of the people I'd miss the most when I left. Then, as Julian and I planned our new life, we received news that slowed everything down.

Although Mum divorced my father before I was even born, she always encouraged me to maintain a relationship with him, which I did. I referred to him as Garry, not Dad. He never had a problem with that—he seemed more a friend than a parent anyway. He took me to rugby league games when I was a child. He'd played the game earlier in his life and remained a dedicated fan of Parramatta. When I was about seven or eight, I made him proud by throwing a hot dog in the face of a Manly supporter. When I told him, in my early thirties, I was gay, he joked that I probably wouldn't want a footy for Christmas.

I admired Garry's approach to life. He had realised as a young adult that being in an office wasn't for him. He spent most of his later years travelling from town to town, farm to farm. I bought him a mobile phone just so I could keep track of his whereabouts. For some of the year, you'd find him picking apples in Batlow and, at other times, sorting mangoes in Bowen. His only possessions were those he could carry. He was a backpacker in his own country, meeting others from all over the world. He made friends in Europe, Asia and South America without ever having to leave our shores. They were drawn to his cheeky sense of humour and ability to outdrink them all. His best mate, Kenny, once told me my old man was invincible.

In late June 2010, we discovered Kenny was wrong. Garry had developed cirrhosis of the liver, no doubt caused by his love of alcohol. Doctors said it was too advanced to fight; they gave him three months at best. Mum told me the news. I'd stopped talking to Garry a few months earlier because I was sick of his drinking. He'd passed through Sydney in March and I was keen for him to meet Julian. He turned up for dinner almost paralytic. I sent him packing while demanding he get sober, for both our sakes.

I called Garry straight after the call from Mum. 'Yeah, not too good,' he calmly told me. Not too good? He could be dead within weeks.

'Why was it too late to fight? What treatment are you on? What are you meant to do now?' My rapid-fire questions all went unanswered—not because he was reluctant to talk, simply because he didn't know the answers.

I was soon on a plane to Far North Queensland so that I could speak directly to his doctor at the Cairns

Base Hospital. It was a hospital I knew well: as a teenager, I was treated there for a broken arm; as a Cairns-based reporter, many years later, I'd visit it regularly for stories. Many of those stories were about a lack of resources—those making decisions in Brisbane often neglected the distant far north.

With Garry sitting beside me, the doctor explained the problem. A transplant would prove useless because the rest of his body was already struggling to function. She expected jaundice to set in soon and toxicity to reach his brain. She said they could pump his stomach and manage his pain, but nothing much else would help, even if he went to a better-equipped hospital down south. Garry smiled at her and quipped, 'All good news then?'

Garry's preference was to stay in Cairns. He liked the weather and knew the people, so, to him, it felt like the perfect place to die. Talking to him about such things was emotionally confronting. I think I saw him as my dad for the first time and felt an overwhelming sense of impending loss.

He suggested he stay in a boarding house he quite liked, but I told him that was out of the question. If he only had a few months left alive, I wanted him to live them in style. I found a penthouse overlooking the marina, and choked up a little when the agent gave me the option of either a three-or six-month lease. I chose to be optimistic and went with the latter.

I'm not certain why I didn't ask for extended leave from work. Perhaps I wasn't strong enough to watch Garry's gradual decline or maybe I worried about what we'd talk about each day. He lived a different life from mine and I wasn't sure how to bridge the gap. I organised for a nurse to make frequent visits and I called every second day. I also flew up twice a month, and we'd usually eat pizza and joke about his neighbours. They didn't know what to make of this tracksuit-wearing hippy on the top floor.

By August, two things had become clear. First, his doctor's timeline was being proven wrong; Garry wasn't showing signs of worsening. Second, we were becoming closer. When I suggested he come to live with Julian and me in Sydney, he didn't think twice.

Despite not knowing how long Garry would be with us, I was still keen to step down from running morning television at Seven. Even if our move to Hong Kong were to be delayed, my frustrations at work were substantial and, I knew, wouldn't disappear.

When Peter Meakin was finally convinced I couldn't be talked out of leaving, attention shifted to who should replace me. My preference was Michael Pell. Michael was a freelance news producer when I hired him at *Sunrise* in 2006. His career path had been somewhat similar to my own, with his having worked in regional TV and at Sky News before ending up at Seven at the age of twenty-four.

He was always going to succeed in television. Even at that age, he knew who to schmooze. He secured an exclusive interview with Bryan Singer in 2006, after befriending the *Superman Returns* director at a party. Some considered it a snub to more seasoned reporters when I allowed Michael to do the interview himself. The fact is, he did a good job.

A similar career path wasn't the only thing Michael and I had in common. In 2007, we were both in long-term and loving relationships with women but we were both questioning our sexuality. That questioning soon led to open flirtation between us.

When we started a relationship later that year, some accused me of predatory behaviour, while others claimed Michael was sleeping his way to the top. Peter Meakin was less judgmental. The wise old owl pulled me aside simply to remind me that workplace romances are fine until they end.

Michael and I had what can only be described as a volatile three-year relationship. There was genuine love between us but it was undermined by jealousy on both our parts. Things weren't made easier by the fact we worked and lived together and that I was the boss (at least at work).

Despite Meakin's concerns, when Michael and I did break up, in 2009, our relationship at work didn't suffer. If anything, it improved—probably because we were having longer periods apart. Around the same time, Michael was put in charge of two of my babies:

Weekend Sunrise and *The Morning Show.* They were promotions that few would dispute he deserved. When the time came in 2010 for me to hand over the reins of *Sunrise,* I wanted Michael to receive them.

Peter Meakin wasn't immediately convinced. He felt we should first look at candidates outside the network. He also wanted to consider former editor of *The Australian Women's Weekly* Robyn Foyster. I'd hired Robyn as a producer the year before, to improve our appeal to women over forty. Her magazine background meant she knew what worked and what didn't. I was clearly a fan, and also her friend, but I think even Robyn would concede she didn't yet have the depth of television experience to run a show like *Sunrise.*

Meakin offered the media a running commentary on the process. He told the *Daily Telegraph* in July: 'Michael Pell is already producing *The Morning Show* and *Weekend Sunrise* and is doing a very good job and is regarded very highly by the network but EP of *Sunrise* is a way off and maybe he would need help if he got Adam's job—which he hasn't at this stage.'

By 'help', he meant a strong second-in-command. Having handpicked the *Sunrise* production team, I didn't share his concern. The producers knew breakfast television like the backs of their hands and were largely responsible for the show's continued success. Despite that, it took until October 2010 for Peter Meakin and David Leckie to give the nod: Michael would take over as executive producer at the end of November.

Before then, I intended to go out with a rather self-indulgent bang. For my final week, we'd broadcast the entire show from the golden sands of Waikiki. We'd taken *Sunrise* to Hawaii once before, in 2005, and I wanted to relive the fun. We booked an entire plane with forty seats for our hosts, producers and crew and the rest for *Sunrise* viewers who'd paid for the right to travel with us. It would also become a family affair, with both my mum and Julian flying over as well (though paying their own way).

The only person missing would be David Koch. A day before we were due to leave Sydney, we got word of an explosion inside a mine on New Zealand's south island. Twenty-nine miners were trapped. Given our experience in Beaconsfield, we knew it might not be a simple task to get them out. It was quickly evolving into a major story, with experts fearing all twenty-nine were dead. That would make it New Zealand's worst mining disaster in almost a century. It would look tasteless if we covered the story while wearing Hawaiian shirts in Waikiki. Just hours before our departure, we made the call to send Kochie to New Zealand instead of him coming to Hawaii.

Splitting up our hosts would make the show harder to produce. Not only would we need to strike a balance between the frivolous and the sombre, we'd be faced with the difficulty of using two separate satellites. Imagine having a conversation with someone who takes up to six seconds to respond to anything you say and you can see what the problem is with satellites. Interaction between Kochie and Mel was bound to be stilted.

Technical challenges weren't going to faze us. The trip to Hawaii was our ticket to party well away from the frenetic pace of our production office in Sydney. We forgot our work roles and just became mates. That meant teasing Natalie Barr when she had cosmetics seized by customs or throwing Jaffas at anyone daring to sleep during the flight. It was like a school camping trip without teachers to keep us in line. The other passengers on the plane were roped in as well. Natalie and Mel offered everyone a lei—an offer that always led to a juvenile level of mirth—while sports presenter Mark Beretta turned hostie, getting drink orders wrong and being the leader in exercises meant to fend off the dreaded deep vein thrombosis.

An advance *Sunrise* team was on hand to greet us at the Hilton Hawaiian Village. They'd been busy turning a honeymoon suite into a mini control room; they removed the beds, to set up a wall of television monitors, and a huge desk with all types of buttons and levers. Our Jetstar pilot thought it looked more complex than his cockpit but it was still a lot smaller than we were used to at home. A typical control room fits up to nine people, including producers, audio and lighting directors and people who, quite literally, call the shots. In Hawaii, only four of us would have to make things work.

The set itself was on a deck overlooking the beach and we had to be careful in positioning our hosts. Mel was placed directly in front of the beach, so viewers would see swimmers and surfers having fun behind her. Natalie was given a more generic background—a tree—so there would be no fear of distractions. There'd be nothing worse than seeing a bloke run around in budgie smugglers while she was reading news about a bombing in Iraq. The hotel's business centre became the *Sunrise* production office but we didn't end up using it all that much. We wrote most of the show late at night, while downing cocktails and feasting on fish at the beachside bar.

The show opened each day with spoofs of classic shows set in Hawaii. We'd parody their opening credits by inserting our own hosts as the key characters. Mark Beretta became Magnum P.I., complete with a ridiculously long moustache and a red Ferrari (or, at least, a convertible rental), Melissa Doyle became Julie, the cruise director, from *The Love Boat,* and Natalie Barr bore a striking resemblance to Mr Roarke from *Fantasy Island.* The *Sunrise* hosts have never been afraid to ham it up and this was as good as it got. When Beretts wasn't Magnum, he was Mr Roarke's off-sider, Tattoo. He crawled around on his knees in an uncanny portrayal that was borderline offensive. No wonder viewers kept asking for an encore.

They weren't the only characters making a splash. The *Sunrise* 'Cash Cow' was our show's unofficial mascot. Our senior editor, Steven Claus, had come up with the idea a few years earlier, as a way of promoting a money giveaway. Since then, the cow costume came with us wherever we went. Production assistants were usually given the job of wearing the suit, meaning the cow's demeanour would match whoever was inside it. Sometimes the cow was particularly outgoing, jumping through the air, dancing around the set and even flirting with the hosts. At other times, it would look half-dead as it faded into the background.

In Hawaii, we renamed the cow 'the *Sunrise* big kahuna' and Julian volunteered to wear it. He took to the role like a new calling in his life. There was something particularly unnerving about seeing my boyfriend dressed as a cow while walking along the beach at Waikiki. He jumped over kids, stumbled into sandcastles and posed for photos with slightly confused tourists. 'Julian the kahuna' even went for a paddle on a traditional Hawaiian outrigger. When the outrigger overturned, we soon discovered that cows couldn't swim. Australians watching from home would have seen a very soggy cow struggling to keep afloat. Like a scene out of *Baywatch* (albeit a very weird episode) lifesavers came to Julian's aid. We cut away just before they took off the cow's head. Julian waded ashore as half-human, half-cow. He collapsed on the sand and declared it was someone else's turn to wear the suit.

The *Sunrise* hosts were as popular in Hawaii as they were back at home. During show time, they'd be surrounded by not only those who'd flown with us from Sydney but by other Aussies who were either holidaying or living around Honolulu. Everyone wanted to hold up signs and ask to say hi to family members down under. One afternoon, I was walking with Mel in town and we were stopped three times by people wanting photos. Natalie, in the meantime, was at the island's biggest shopping centre. End-of-year sales had just begun, so she ended buying more cosmetics than she had had seized at the airport.

Time differences between Australia and Hawaii meant we weren't on air until just before lunch, local time. I usually had breakfast with Mum and Julian down by the pool before taking a casual stroll to our honeymoon control room. Here was the very definition of a working holiday.

It wasn't so relaxed all the time, though.

Weather presenter Grant Denyer had brought his new wife, Cheryl, who also happened to be his producer. Midway through our Wednesday show in Hawaii, a live cross to Grant on the roof of the Hilton dropped out. We were left with black on the screen and had to scramble back to our main hosts ahead of time. I was in the control room and lashed out at Cheryl over our production intercom. It had been her job to investigate the live-cross location the day before, to ensure it worked.

Minutes later, Grant stormed into the control room and looked as if he were about to punch me. His face turned red as he levelled abuse, accusing me of insulting his wife. In reality, I had spoken to her like I would have to any other producer who'd let the show down. There's no time for niceties while we're live on air. Things often get tense but that's part of the deal.

I instructed him to leave but the yelling continued. Members of the crew were left stunned as they heard it unfold on the production intercom. Here was the weather presenter and executive producer engaged in a screaming match while our happy little breakfast show was still on air. Director Paul Slater was struggling to hear the show, so also started yelling, in a desperate appeal for calm. In the end, production manager Dave Masala broke up the exchange by physically stepping in. Dave's not a small guy, so when he pushed us apart it had the desired effect. Grant slammed the door on his way out. He was off air for the rest of the morning (I can't remember if that was his choice or mine) leaving Mel to read the weather.

A week after we returned home, Grant sent me a note. It turned out there'd been a problem with Cheryl's phone in Hawaii that meant she missed many emails from the producers and me. This included the request to investigate the live-cross location that eventually failed. Grant told me, 'No wonder you got so frustrated. While I truly wish it never happened at all, I thought you were taking an explosive pot shot at Chezzi for no reason.' I hold no grudge against him or Cheryl. As he would often say, he is a husband first and presenter second. That can cause problems when partners work together but, hey, who am I to judge?

The week in Hawaii marked the end of my nine years as head of the *Sunrise* family. On the flight back, I started to reflect on the things we'd achieved since setting up shop in an old tin shed and, in particular, the many times we'd made a real difference to people's lives. Television should never be used just to make money; it's a powerful platform that can help shape public thinking. In between the big-name performances and high-profile stunts, *Sunrise* had done something much more important: we'd helped 'Spread the Love'. Our critics often belittled that slogan but it was at the heart of everything we did. It meant using the show to help send fresh water to townships in Cambodia. It meant being the driving force behind the tsunami relief concert. It meant sending a plane full of tradies to help repair cyclone-ravaged Far North Queensland. Most of all, it meant connecting with everyday people. Listening to them, rather than lecturing them, was our most important act.

I was proud of our achievements but no less relieved to be putting the show behind me. Breakfast television is rewarding but relentless. With Garry still sick at home, it was time for me to have a shift in my priorities. I was looking forward to sleeping in and starting the next chapter of my life.

15

COURTING TROUBLE

Seven months after being told he was terminally ill, my father was about to see something he didn't think he would: 2011.

For the past few years, Julian and I had hosted New Year's Eve parties at my mum's place in Circular Quay. Her unit had a prized view of the Harbour Bridge but she hardly used it after moving permanently to Vanuatu. Our soirees were often the source of scandalous rumour; there were stories of drunken orgies, drug taking and naked violin players. For the record, the violin players were always fully clothed.

On the final night of 2010, Garry sat in the corner and just took everything in—a permanent smirk plastered on his face. He told me I had some interesting friends, while watching two guys who'd just met make out in Mum's kitchen. As the clock wound down, neither of us knew how long *he* had left. His condition had weakened but not to the point of being a major concern. His doctors said he was clearly a fighter, meaning they were no longer willing to forecast the ending. He fell asleep right after the fireworks. Perhaps that's just as well. There are some things no parent should see.

***

Julian and I started 2011 with an unexpected sense of uncertainty. We couldn't just turn our backs on Garry and, besides, our bid for the unit in Hong Kong had been rejected. Julian reasoned that maybe it was fate. His architectural business was starting to expand and he was even taking on new staff. We still wanted to be in Hong Kong but accepted we would need to wait.

Fearing that outcome, I'd kept a foot inside Channel Seven. For two days a week, I'd become a consultant. I considered it a fairly meaningless role but that didn't matter. I gave advice to Michael Pell when needed. He talked through many decisions with me, no matter how minor they seemed. The fact was, he was getting it right more often than not, but perhaps he felt better knowing I agreed with him.

When I wasn't lending Michael a hand, I was helping advertisers pervade TV shows. James Warburton was in charge of Seven's sales team. He was a man I liked and had been close to ever since he helped get *The Morning Show* on air, back in 2007. James thought it would be a good idea to have a producer in the room when his team pitched ideas to major clients. There was increasing demand to subtly integrate products into programs, rather than hope viewers would pay attention to commercial breaks. These days, of course, the process is about as subtle as a drag queen in a nunnery; some shows dedicate more time to sponsors than to content.

Back at home, Garry was playing host to what seemed like a never-ending stream of pilgrims. Word had got around the farms that he was seriously ill, so many of his mates wanted one last hurrah. Like him, most were nomads, so dropped in while passing through Sydney. I had mixed feelings about their visits. He was always happy to see them but conversations inevitably turned morbidly awkward when it came to saying goodbye. Julian had promised his family we'd spend early February with them in Hong Kong, so that we'd be there for Chinese New Year. Garry insisted we go and even joked that he'd stay alive until we returned. We arranged for a friend to stay with him for the week we'd be gone.

While in Hong Kong, Julian introduced me to a traditional Asian bathhouse. They vary from country to country. In Korea, they're known as *jimjilbangs* and are firmly embedded in the culture. Japan has its more intimate *sentos* or *onsens,* while parts of China offer a hybrid of both. Getting me to visit took some convincing, as it would require me to be naked in front of a group of strangers. That was intimidating enough but I was also likely to be the only *gweilo* (Cantonese for 'foreigner' or 'ghost man'), so was bound to stand out.

Once inside, I realised no one could care less about me. I ditched my inhibitions and took a plunge in steaming hot water of around forty degrees. Actually, it was less a plunge than an inch-by-inch creep. Just as my body got used to the hot water, Julian urged me to jump straight into cold water. Water torture I feared, but did as instructed. It was like nothing I'd felt before, as my senses went into a spin. Such a simple process that didn't just cleanse my skin but seemed to free my mind. I'd found my nirvana hidden in a backstreet of smoggy Hong Kong.

We got talking about it on the plane back to Australia, and Julian revealed he used to visit a similar place in Sydney. It was known as the Ginseng Bathhouse and was apparently a Kings Cross institution. The mere mention of a bathhouse in the Cross would lead you to think it was nothing more than a den of sin, but Julian assured me (with a hint of disappointment) that it was the real deal. The bathhouse operated on the first floor of the Crest Hotel for almost twenty years. It closed in 2008, when the hotel was sold for redevelopment.

The Ginseng Bathhouse had been the only Asian-style bathhouse in Sydney and had proved so popular that you'd often struggle to get in on weekends. It attracted not just Asians but inner-city hipsters. Even stay-at-home mums from the eastern suburbs would sit around naked while sipping champagne. In the week of its closure, the *Sydney Morning Herald* lamented: 'Sydney's bathhouse devotees were in shock. None of the smart, expensive la-de-da spa treatments that have become the latest craze could ever replace it.'

The more I talked about the bathhouse, the more people I met who missed it. From television host Andrew O'Keefe to News Limited's former CEO Kim Williams, everyone seemed to have a story about Ginseng. Could their happy memories translate to a happy future for me? Naked ambition maybe, but it soon became my mission to bring the Ginseng Bathhouse back from the dead.

***

On the second day of March in 2011, James Warburton did the unthinkable. The man everyone thought would soon be running Channel Seven instead agreed to become the next chief executive of the much smaller Network Ten.

Warburton was one of the most successful sales executives in the country long before he joined Channel Seven in 2003. While running the media agency Universal McCann Australia in the late 1990s, he snared big spending clients like Coles Myer and the federal government. A decade later at Seven, he would command the biggest share of revenue in commercial television.

In October 2010, Warburton started to renegotiate his contract at Seven. After serving his time as head of sales, he was angling for a bigger role and that could mean only one thing: CEO. His problem was that

Seven already had one of those and David Leckie showed no signs of abdicating.

Just before 9am on Saturday, 28 February 2011, Warburton arrived in the exclusive Sydney suburb of Darling Point. He was about to meet Kerry Stokes at the tycoon's harbourside mansion. Stokes knew he was at risk of losing Warburton unless he could guarantee him a career path.

While chatting over coffee, Stokes told Warburton he would become Seven's head of television on 1 July. A newly created position, it was not the one Warburton wanted. Stokes then delivered the silver lining. He assured him he'd be CEO within twelve months. Leckie wouldn't be leaving the business but would focus on a broader management role at Seven West Media—the umbrella group overseeing Stokes's various companies. In the best news of all, Leckie had apparently agreed to the change.

There are two different versions of what happened next. The Stokes camp claims Warburton then shook hands on the deal. Warburton says he agreed but with one condition. He wanted first to look Leckie in the eye, in order truly to believe he'd get his support.

Later that day, Warburton and his wife, Nikki, (also a media executive) had lunch with Lachlan and Sarah Murdoch at the Murdochs' home in Vaucluse. Warburton insists the lunch was prearranged but the timing certainly proved helpful. Lachlan Murdoch was then acting chief executive of Network Ten and was on the hunt for his permanent replacement. He knew that luring Warburton to Ten would be a coup. Warburton told Murdoch about his conversation with Stokes and said his future at Seven would all come down to a meeting with Leckie on Monday. By the end of lunch, it was clear to Warburton that he had another option if he didn't like what Leckie had to say.

Warburton walked into the office that he hoped would soon be his just after 2pm on Monday. According to a later affidavit, this is the conversation he claims he then had with David Leckie:

Warburton: Hi David.

Leckie: Here comes Mr Ambitious. I've been kicked into touch. I've been retired. How sad.

Warburton: Mate, you're a great supporter, clearly.

Leckie: So you've heard what the Chairman wants to do? How much he wants to pay you?

Warburton: Yes. We discussed it on Saturday.

Leckie: So?

Warburton: Well, what do you think?

Leckie: It's sad. I'm being retired.

246

Warburton: Well, you and I need to work out a plan as to how we will work together. If we can't do that, there is no point. I have no future here if my boss won't support me.

Leckie: I have to do it. Stokes has told me I have to step aside and make some room. I'm tired. I do have to support it.

Warburton: So what's the plan and how will it work?

Leckie: I don't know.

Warburton: Great, no point.

Leckie: I'm 60 soon. This is all yours now.

Warburton: Mate, the Seven West deal made you look like a king. You are around, it's not that bad. But if we can't work together then it will be a futile exercise. I can't take a job when I have no power.

Leckie: Mate, I have counted that between Nine and Seven, I've been a CEO for 20 years. I'm tired. It's time. I have no choice. I will still be involved though. I will not leave my office. I will still call people. I will still call the shots. I am the frigging boss of the fuckwits at WAN [West

Australian Newspapers]. I'll fix them right up. It will take me five minutes to fix the idiots on the WAN board. They are fucking dopes. They wouldn't know a thing about television, they don't even get how to put a paper together. They just do what Kerry tells them. Fuck me, Western Australia.

Warburton: Mate, there is no point. Unless I have your honest support which I didn't think I did, and now I know I don't, I will just piss off.

Leckie: Over with Lachlan?

Warburton: Mate, I'm yours to lose. You've effectively lost me.

On Wednesday, 2 March, at 10am. James Warburton signed a contract to become the next chief executive of Channel Ten.

***

In the meantime, Julian and I spent almost two months looking for a new venue for the Ginseng Bathhouse. It wasn't easy. We needed somewhere with ample room, good access and that was, preferably, close to the old bathhouse location, so as to easily attract its old loyalists. We found the perfect space in the basement of the boutique Diamant Hotel on Kings Cross Road. We negotiated a lease, on this empty shell of 800 square metres, that wouldn't kick in until the end of June 2012, giving us plenty of time to scope the project.

Julian knew it would be anything but simple. There were no other bathhouses of this kind in Australia, meaning building contractors would have limited expertise. Heath regulations had also changed since the days of Ginseng, so we'd need to overcome significant hurdles to get approval. If we were going to commit, Julian would need to turn down other clients for at least twelve months, to oversee the design and business planning. He'd require structural, mechanical and hydraulic engineers, and he'd need local consultants to help win approval from council and state health authorities.

We had another problem: banks refused to fund the scope. Some feared we were planning some form of gay sex club, while others called it too much of a risk, especially given there weren't any similar businesses with which to compare it. The old bathhouse (to which we now owned its name and databases) hadn't kept clear financial records.

We had to make a call on whether we'd fund it ourselves.

We both felt passionate about Ginseng but for different reasons. Julian saw it as the ultimate test of his architectural skills. It would challenge him in a way that residential projects never could. For me, I hoped it would kick-start a life away from television. I believed in the business and knew others would too.

We threw caution to the wind and just hit go. The first thing we needed was $200000 to secure a guarantee over the Diamant basement. That would keep it off the market for a year while we worked on the plan. With Julian turning away clients and me only working two days a week, we desperately needed extra cash. As the banks weren't any help, I'd need to return to full-time work.

I really didn't want it to be at Channel Seven. As much as I'd enjoyed my time there, I knew there was nothing more I could do at the network. Michael Pell was now operating under his own steam and, if anything, was keen to step out of my shadow. That left the rather unattractive prospect of helping advertisers each day. There was potentially one other option: could James Warburton's defection to Ten also allow me to escape?

Given my relationship with Warburton, I suspected I could convince him to take me with him and for a role outside of breakfast television. But there was a hitch. Channel Seven wasn't at all thrilled by Warburton's plan to depart. According to one account, Kerry Stokes even phoned Lachlan Murdoch and declared: 'I'm going to kill your company. I'm going to fucking kill it.' Seven launched immediate court action to frustrate Ten's plans. Ten wanted Warburton to take up his new post on 14 July 2011. Seven argued that, under the terms of a management equity scheme, he couldn't make the switch until October 2012.

That meant James couldn't yet act on Ten's behalf and even if he could, I couldn't approach him because of my own obligations to Seven. I didn't think that freeing myself of those obligations would prove difficult; I was only at the network two days a week and was doing very little. My assessment was naive. Given the wider battle being waged with Warburton and my known association with him, my sudden request to break ties with Seven was always going to raise eyebrows. I was told I'd need to stay.

I felt frustrated and trapped. Julian was depending on me to find extra money for Ginseng and I'd been excited by the prospect of doing something else. I felt I had no choice but to seek the viewpoints of lawyers. Court action seemed my only hope.

I had very mixed emotions. I certainly wanted to leave and join Ten but the thought of suing Seven was difficult to deal with. It had been the network I'd loved since childhood. The place where I'd made my name.

There was also a time pressure. I was due to fly out with the *Sunrise* team on Friday, to help with the coverage of Prince William's marriage to Kate Middleton in London. I was reluctant to have Seven pay for my business-class seats and ritzy hotel room, only to have me return to Australia and take them to court. I thought it was only fair to make up my mind before then.

After Seven's final refusal to release me, I gave my lawyers the green light. My claim was lodged with the Federal Court on Thursday, 21 April, and Seven served with papers shortly afterwards. Despite my dramatic action, Peter Meakin told me to continue on the trip to London.

The news hadn't leaked when we boarded the flight at Sydney Airport the following morning. The plane wasn't just carrying the *Sunrise* team but the hosts of Channel Nine's *Today* and even Kerri-Anne Kennerley. I sat next to Michael, who felt I had an obligation to tell David Koch and Melissa Doyle before they heard about it from somebody else. I did that while having a drink with them in the bar of the Qantas A380. 'Fuck,' was Kochie's frank, and pretty accurate, assessment. Mel was supportive and said I had to do what was right for me.

By the time the plane touched down for a stopover in Singapore, my legal offensive had been splashed across Australian news websites. The *Daily Telegraph* had spoken to Peter Meakin: 'I'm incredibly saddened that someone I have worked with and the network has nurtured is suddenly and prematurely taking us to court,' he was quoted as saying. I was as sad as he was. The *Australian* linked my action to James Warburton, writing 'the cases highlight the friction among executives at Seven over succession. Mr Warburton wanted chief executive David Leckie's job while Mr Boland sought the top job at news and public affairs, held by Peter Meakin'. I was feeling down

...é we were at Singapore Airport but found solace ,rom the most unlikely of people.

Today hosts Karl Stefanovic and Lisa Wilkinson had been my rivals for almost four years. In truth, though, I liked them both very much and still considered Lisa a friend after her days at *Weekend Sunrise.* I ran into them while heading back to the plane and got to talking about all manner of things—everything except the court case. We were talking so much that we ended up at the wrong side of the terminal. Assuming the role of the strict mother, Lisa quickly ushered us back, but Karl and I kept gossiping five steps behind. He again told me of his desire to host a primetime talk show and figured I'd be perfect to produce it. It was something he'd raised once before, during another random encounter. I didn't take it overly seriously; I suspected Karl said the same thing to many of his producer mates.

The leg from Singapore to London was much more fun than the one from Sydney. Everyone had too much to drink and reminisced about the good old days of television. Nobody was better at that than Kerri-Anne Kennerley, who was, as always, incredibly engaging. After a champagne or two, she offered me a timely piece of wisdom: the only person you need to be loyal to in television is yourself.

The mid-flight media love-in made the gossip pages at home after a fellow passenger claimed we'd monopolised the bar, which was probably true. The same source accused Stefanovic of making an 'arse' of himself. He was said to have stumbled from the plane after discovering his 'lost' mobile phone inside his shoe. Again, probably true. When I came to Stefanovic's defence on Twitter, the *Daily Telegraph* speculated that I was fishing for a new gig at Channel Nine. That wasn't true.

At any rate, everyone loves a royal wedding. At least, that's what journos kept telling their readers and viewers. More than 7000 members of the global media had sought accreditation. Our security passes (which struck me as pretty easy to fake) gave us access to otherwise closed streets. Many parts of the city were in lockdown as police prepared for an invasion. A million people were expected to line the processional route from Westminster Abbey to Buckingham Palace.

Many television crews were housed in a temporary compound directly opposite the palace. It really was something to see. Time differences throughout the world meant the twenty-two glass-fronted studios were lit up around the clock. Each studio was no more than 10 square metres but they all had what producers would call the money shot—a direct line of sight to the palace balcony, where we expected to see the traditional post-wedding kiss.

Channel Seven didn't just have one of the mini studios, but a prized hosting position on the edge of St James's Park, within spitting distance of the Victoria Memorial outside the Palace gates. This gave a better sense of the atmosphere, because it was at ground level and was open air, and was the position we mainly used for *Sunrise* in the days leading up to the wedding. As Mel and Kochie were on air each night (London time), a crowd would gather behind them, waving Australian flags. Soon enough, they'd start chanting *Aussie Aussie Aussie, oi oi oi!* Our viewers weren't the only ones to hear them. A Canadian show was on air right beside us and the anchor was heard to say, 'You can always count on Aussies to make a noise.'

On the day of the wedding itself, *Sunrise* staffer Dacien Hadland, Melissa Doyle and I decided to brave the crowd crush along The Mall. Saying we were nuts, our colleagues preferred to stick to the relative comfort of the media's exclusive compound. We entered The Mall from near Trafalgar Square and spent at least three hours weaving our way towards the Palace. It was an extraordinary experience. I'm no monarchist but it was hard not to appreciate the sense of history that was everywhere.

Police had set up barricades every 100 metres, meaning sections of the crowd were penned in. And penned in tightly. This wasn't the place for anyone with a fear of intimacy (or body odour). We only got through thanks to our media passes. At each barricade, the bobbies were left perplexed by why we'd come the hard way. We reached the palace just in time to see the much-hyped first public kiss. Mel seemed more excited about that than either Dacien or I.

**

When I got back to Australia, the legal stoush with Channel Seven had become much fiercer. Both sides were trading narky letters by the day and sometimes by the hour. I figured Seven was trying to make the exercise as expensive as possible for me by constantly requesting legal responses to relatively trivial issues. It had deeper pockets and a bigger team of lawyers and in any test of endurance, would come out in front.

In early May, Kerry Stokes asked me to meet with him at his private office in Woolloomooloo; those at Seven call it The Villa. I'd been there only once before, for breakfast inside his remarkable map room. Stokes values history and some of his Australian maps dated back to pre-Federation. I knew this meeting would be much less pleasant than when we shared eggs on toast but he still showed me warmth as we sat down. I've never known Stokes not to be respectful. I hoped to make him understand why I wanted to leave but the meeting did little to change things.

**

It coincided with something much worse that was happening at home. At the beginning of May, my father's condition had deteriorated sharply. He could no longer climb steps on his own and seemed unable to make eye contact. His already yellowed skin was often now bleeding. I tried to convince him to be admitted to hospital, as Julian and I felt useless at managing his pain. Garry continued to refuse to go.

By 9 May, he could hardly talk. Late in the day, I heard a loud thump; he'd fallen halfway down the stairs. I tried to get him back on what were now his last legs while Julian called an ambulance. Just before it arrived, Garry managed to look me in the eye to say, 'Don't let me die.'

He passed away in the early hours of 12 May 2011 at the Canterbury Hospital. He was fifty-eight. That's a day I now mark each year, both because of his death and because it is my mother's birthday.

***

By June, it was obvious to me that Seven believed I wanted to set up a rival show to *Sunrise*. I couldn't think of anything worse. Breakfast television was the last place I wanted to be and I tried to convince them of that. But as the battle continued, so did the stress.

One of the key reasons for me wanting to switch to Ten was to raise quick money for our bathhouse project. The legal saga had now placed the entire project in jeopardy.

I was starting to soften my stance, accepting I'd need to stay at Seven, but maintained I wanted my primary focus to be on something other than morning TV. By then, I'd become a passionate advocate of social media. I believed Seven still had a long way to go before properly embracing the brave new world.

On 27 July, Seven announced that my lawsuit had been dropped and declared me the network's new director of social media.

16

BEFORE SUNSET

In January 2006, Channel Seven jumped into bed with internet giant Yahoo. Seven felt, quite rightly, that to survive in the multimedia age, it would need the expertise and audience reach of an online pro.

Yahoo!7 operated as a separate company and in a separate building from Channel Seven, but took control of all of Seven's websites, including social media. Come mid-2011, it was becoming clear that my new title of Seven's director of social media was just that—a title. I'd been trapped inside television's metaphorical warehouse with very little to do. The only way out was to focus on something that no longer excited me: *Sunrise.*

The show was under significant ratings pressure and had been for two years. At one point in 2009, Nine's chief executive, David Gyngell, cheekily sent me a neck brace, so I wouldn't get hurt 'rubbernecking' *Today.* Our biggest weakness was Melbourne—in part, because of *Today'* s Lisa Wilkinson. Research revealed that Victorians liked the way she stood up to her co-host Karl Stefanovic and believed Mel Doyle looked passive by comparison. They didn't necessarily blame her—Mel's personal popularity rating remained high.

It was more a case of the Kochie and Mel partnership appearing increasingly out of balance. As *Today* continued to gain ground, I even thought about quarantining Melbourne from the rest of the country. In my rather unrealistic thought bubble, the city would get its own edition of *Sunrise,* with its very own hosts. We'd base the show somewhere overtly Melbourne, like the boardwalk in front of Crown Casino. So, my production team would prepare two separate shows each day—one for Melbourne and one for the rest of the country. I even toyed with all sorts of names, from Steve Vizard to Jennifer Keyte, to host the Melbourne edition. In the end, my bubble was burst when I considered the costs.

A key reason for me wanting to leave my post in 2010 was so someone else could inject new ideas into the show. It needed a leader who wasn't tired of breakfast television and would be up for a fight, just as I had been almost a decade earlier. I suspect that Michael knew when he stepped into the role that the strength of the presenting line-up was under question. Mel and Kochie had formed one of the great partnerships of Australian television, and without them, *Sunrise* would never have claimed the breakfast crown. But television shows have a lifespan, and unless things are shaken up, people lose interest. At some point, Kochie and Mel would need to separate. 'There was a feeling that it was time to freshen up the line-up,' says Peter Meakin.

Wanting to make a switch didn't mean we thought one or both of the hosts had reached a use-by date. Any change would guarantee them new and potentially higher-profile network roles. The question was: what form should that change take?

Our chief executive, recalls Meakin, had a very firm view: 'all the research on *Sunrise* showed that people loved Mel and it was Kochie who polarised people. That was the research that you and I used to see. The view was taken by David Leckie that "Bugger the research, it's not worth a burnt pie. Kochie is the heart and soul of the show and I don't give a fuck what the research shows, Kochie is untouchable."

Kochie had polarised people since the day *Sunrise* began but that clearly hadn't hurt our ratings. Some watched because they loved him and some watched because they hated him. The absence of any middle ground was a major factor in the show's success.

Should Mel be the one to leave, my preference was to replace her with Natalie Barr. She sat in for Mel whenever she took holidays and always added a new dimension. She was never afraid to share her thoughts—including, strangely, a hatred for cats—and was well liked by the *Sunrise* audience.

I felt that Michael disagreed. He'd become close to Samantha Armytage while producing *Weekend Sunrise* and I figure saw her as destined for stardom. He was no doubt right but, to me, that didn't mean she was destined for *Sunrise*. The weekday show was never about stars but about people who cared about making a difference.

I then threw my support behind *The Morning Show* host Kylie Gillies, who had similar qualities to Natalie's—she was smart, savvy and funny. I proposed that Natalie take Kylie's old role alongside Larry Emdur on *The Morning Show* and that Monique Wright become the new *Sunrise* newsreader. The research and ratings trends worried me, and I pushed for change to happen by the end of the year. I never once stopped to think I might be hurting long-time friends like Kochie or Mel. My priority was to help the show.

As Michael waited for movement, he got on with changing what he could straightaway. The show's content became much more tabloid. More emphasis was placed on celebrities and less on risky unknowns. Pet causes were sidelined in favour of stories that would play well with the mainstream.

Although I disliked this direction, it was the right one to take. This reminded me why I could no longer be the show's executive producer.

***

Julian was making good progress on the architectural drawings for Ginseng. His concepts were beautiful, but expensive. An independent assessment put the cost of construction just shy of $4 million. I told him to push on (despite not knowing where we'd find the money). This was our passion project and we were determined to see it through. Any money I was making at Seven was used to cover our mounting bills. There were engineers, consultants and designers to pay, and most charged by the hour.

We had until the end of July 2012 to come up with the millions needed for the actual build. If we missed that date, we'd be locked in to a fifteen-year lease that we might not be able to service. The deadline was just over seven months away.

***

While I was happy to use Seven as a cash cow, I was still frustrated by my actual work (or lack thereof). My social-media tasks were negligible and I'd given about as much advice as I could on *Sunrise*. To keep myself occupied, I proposed taking control of one of my old shows, *Weekend Sunrise*. It had been without an executive producer since Michael moved on. Both he and Meakin agreed to me taking over.

While Michael added his tabloid touch to *Sunrise*, I set about removing it from weekends. I stripped back entertainment-heavy segments and ditched loud-mouthed Hollywood 'correspondents'—many of whom did little more than read internet site *TMZ* before coming on air to regurgitate it. (Nelson Aspen, who reports on showbiz for the weekday show, is a rare exception.) I wasn't planning to replicate Channe

Nine's old *Sunday* show. First, we didn't have those kinds of resources. Second, we had to maintain a more engaging, *Sunrise* feel. We would still be a largely talk-based format but it would be a different conversation than before.

As with everything I did, I couldn't help but encourage fanfare; I wanted the audience to know that *Weekend Sunrise* was changing. Michael agreed to run promos during the weekday show, and we made a big deal of the new format in blogs and press releases.

All was set for a relaunch on Saturday, 5 November 2011.

Two hours before going on air, the unthinkable happened: there was a technical meltdown. We couldn't access any of our pictures, which would mean a news bulletin without vision. We couldn't even do live crosses. All we'd have for three hours would be four hosts sitting around a desk, talking to each other.

In all my time at Seven, I'd never seen such a crippling malfunction.

Ten minutes before our scheduled start, I made a call I would later regret. I told network control that *Weekend Sunrise* wouldn't be going on air and asked them to run standby programming instead. Ironically, they chose to air back-to-back episodes of *Beyond 2000*—a show dedicated to the wonders of technology.

On any other day, I would have gone on air and just winged it. I think I was so conscious of the fact that people would be passing judgment on the so-called new format, that I preferred for them to see nothing at all.

It's fair to say that Kerry Stokes didn't agree and later did something astounding. He handed me a letter dated 26 October 1996—it was addressed to him and signed by me. It was the letter I'd sent him while still a junior producer at Sky; he'd held on to it for fifteen years. He referred me specifically to one line: 'You can't afford to have one problem when you're up against news on every other channel.'

He then asked, 'Do you think you have lived up to your own standard?'

The most powerful media tycoon in the country had just used my own words to dress me down. That was the last time we ever spoke.

***

It was March 2012 and we'd raised almost $3 million for Ginseng. Much of that had come from the sale of our house and from relatives prepared to risk their savings. If we didn't raise the remaining $1 million by July, we'd have to make a call on whether to pull the pin. If we pushed ahead and still couldn't bridge the gap, our families could lose their money.

The uncertainty was hard to deal with. I feared not only the impact on our relatives but Julian's inevitable disappointment if the project didn't proceed. He'd spent a year producing the most complicated set of drawings I'd ever seen. He worked on them seven days a week and long after I fell asleep each night.

We turned to crowd funding and government grants, and even flirted with dodgy loan sharks. I also sat down with David Koch. He offered advice on securing private investors and considered buying a stake himself. In the end, it was all too late. A week before our deadline, we scrapped the project. Julian and I lost more than $500000. Nobody else lost a cent, though.

It was an awful situation. Not only was I still at a network that had refused to let me leave but the light at the end of the tunnel had just been switched off. Even if I could escape, what point would it serve? And my bank account was now all but empty.

I tried my best to seek solace in *Weekend Sunrise*. Some executives, including Michael, felt that I was using the show to preach a left-wing agenda. This was true to some extent but, to me, it was warranted, given many other media outlets had moved so far to the right. I led a small but passionate team of producers; their enthusiasm helped restore mine. They'd pitch stories about equality, climate change and Syria. We'd host performances from the likes of Korean pianist Yiruma and political activist John Butler. We even put buskers on air.

The hosts were inspiring. Simon Reeve, for example, was perhaps the most compassionate man I knew.

One of my favourite moments of the show was watching him report from Brisbane on the lantern walk for refugees. He took the time to meet people Australia had saved from persecution, and described their optimism and genuine gratitude for being given a new home, before declaring:

> I know that even as this story goes to air, there are people poised to send us emails and texts full of hate. But these are the faces of Australia in 2012. And we should be very proud that we have given these people a safe and secure home because in every way, they make Australia a better place to live in.

He was right. We did get complaints. Such was the climate in Australia.

Weekend Sunrise was never afraid to challenge merchants of hatred. The show allocated thirty minutes (an extraordinary length of time by commercial TV standards) for an interview with far-right Dutch politician Geert Wilders. Andrew O'Keefe, as a former lawyer, carefully dissected Wilders's offensive case against Islam and, by its very nature, Muslims.

It ended with this gem.

> Andrew: Your failure to see the comparisons between Muslim people and non-Muslim people shows a lack of wisdom and certainly a lack of compassion or perhaps it's just wilful blindness.

Wilders: If people in Australia are as ignorant as you are, you will have a very tough time in the future.

Rather, if more people in Australia were like Andrew O'Keefe, our future would only be bright.

***

My contract was finally up at the beginning of 2013 and, for the first time in years, I was reluctant to leave. Where would I go? Ginseng hadn't happened but the dent in our bank account had. Producing the weekend show might have been Off-Broadway but it was easy money. Besides, I adored the team and believed in the content.

I started talking to and actively lobbying Seven for a new contract, and would have signed, had it not been for a visit from my former partner (and former *Sunrise* producer) Yoko Shimizu. She was in Australia to attend a wedding and took me out to lunch. She couldn't believe I was planning to stay and accused me of becoming complacent. Worse still, she said I'd lost my passion.

It was the wake-up call I needed. By the time we got to dessert, my mind was made up. I emailed Seven from the restaurant to tell them I was leaving.

'Well, that comes as a bit of a surprise,' was Meakin's one-sentence response. To him *and* to Julian, who asked what the plan now was. I had absolutely no idea.

I walked out the door at Seven for the final time on Thursday, 28 February 2013. It felt very different from when I first walked in, fourteen years earlier—Seven had become just another workplace. I had a few drinks with mates and then headed home. I was relieved to have left the network behind me.

17

COUNTING TO TEN

I've long been a believer in fate. When Channel Ten sacked me in 1999, the door opened at Channel Seven. And had Seven not scrapped plans for a major breakfast show in 2002, the cult of Kochie and Mel may never have happened.

The day after Yoko convinced me to leave my TV home, I received a phone call from executive recruiter Paul Anstee. He wouldn't tell me who he was working for but asked whether I might be available for a chat. I arrived at his terrace-cum-office in Balmain to be greeted by his client: the chief executive of Fox Sports, Patrick Delany. We'd never met but I knew him by reputation. He'd been a key player in the success of Foxtel and was a favourite of then News Limited boss Kim Williams.

A former litigator and competitive swimmer, Delany is fond of winning. But he had a problem. He knew that Australia's love for pay television could cool as internet speeds increased and viewers found better content at a cheaper price. He still had one major advantage: the broadcast rights to many of Australia's most popular sports. But he wanted to find other ways to innovate; other ways to get people talking about, and therefore wanting, Fox Sports.

Delany was sounding me out for a role that could help him meet that challenge. The more he talked, the more I wanted to work for him. I liked his record, I liked his drive and I liked his strategic thinking.

There was only one problem: I knew nothing about sport.

Delany assured me that didn't necessarily rule me out, conceding his own knowledge of sport wasn't as great as I might think. 'Do you know the name of the Australian cricket captain?' I asked. 'Because if you do, you already know more than me.'

Fate was starting to look shaky.

Meeting Paul Anstee proved useful, though. Reserved by nature (particularly alongside the imposing Patrick Delany), Paul still managed to be extremely well connected. He threw me in front of media bosses all over town, including Garry Linnell at Fairfax—the man who had had to resign from Channel Nine when his job was offered to me. 'So, you've come to do me out of another gig?' he joked as we sat down.

The meeting I cared most about was with the chief executive of FremantleMedia, Ian Hogg. The production company had a major presence in Asia, imposing franchises like *The X Factor* on people from India to Japan. Not only was Hogg in charge of Fremantle's Asian footprint, he knew the region well, having founded a media company in Singapore. I wanted his help to get me out of Australia.

When I first met him, he offered me one of his homemade muffins (and later emailed me the recipe) before telling me to drink more water. He sounded more like a naturopath than a major player in global television and instantly felt like a mentor. He'd achieved so much that there was no need for him to be arrogant, and he seemed to get genuine pleasure from helping others shine. I envied those on his team. We talked through my options. Sure, there was Asia, and he was happy to hook me up with his people, but what about at home? I told him I'd kept in contact with James Warburton after he became chief executive of Channel Ten.

Even though Ten had cancelled a breakfast show just a few months earlier, James was reluctant to completely abandon the slot. And with good reason. Having been at Seven, he knew the power of a breakfast show in setting the tone for a network's entire brand. I was fond of calling the breakfast show the front door to a network. Beyond that, it can play a major role in boosting primetime ratings. There's a reason both *Sunrise* and *Today* hosts spend significant (and to me, too much) time talking about shows like *My Kitchen Rules* and *The Voice.* Research confirms a direct correlation with how those shows are perceived and how they are talked about in the morning shows. Breakfast also punches above its weight in attracting the attention of advertisers. Jetstar is a good example. The airline gets a lot more value from David Koch announcing its discounted fares than from running a traditional commercial. And it's willing to pay a significant premium for that value. And, finally, breakfast shows serve as an ideal breeding ground for talent. Almost every presenter from *Sunrise*, including David Koch, Melissa Doyle, Samantha Armytage, Edwina Bartholomew, Grant Denyer, Mark Beretta, James Tobin and Simon Reeve, have had their own primetime shows following their morning stints. To me, a network without a breakfast show is like a pie without sauce. You can get away with it, but it's never as good.

I told Hogg that if Ten re-entered the space, they'd need to find younger viewers than those who watch *Sunrise* and *Today.* One of the reasons Ten had failed with its most recent breakfast show was that it tried to capture that same audience. They stood no chance against the big, established brands: *Today* and *Sunrise* already fought tooth and nail every single morning and weren't going to take kindly to an upstart treading on their turf. Ten, I argued, should keep its eye firmly on the audience it knew best: those aged under fifty.

Back in 2007, I produced a *Sunrise* concert at Currumbin Beach on the Gold Coast that had stayed in my mind ever since. Thousands of people lined the sand as Aussie band Powderfinger belted out their hits. It wasn't just beautiful television but also uniquely Australian. A beach struck me as the perfect place to host a breakfast show that was trying to catch the attention of a younger audience. It would look completely different from its studio-based rivals and convey an element of fun.

The choice of hosts would be just as crucial. A key ingredient in the success of *Sunrise* was the ability of Kochie and Mel to connect to middle Australia. If Ten wanted to reach a different generation, it would need people who spoke its language.

James Mathison and Maude Garrett were regular guests on *Weekend Sunrise* and, to me, fit the bill. James was a former host of *Australia Idol* but his knowledge extended beyond pop culture. He has a strong social conscience that I knew would resonate with the target market. Peter Garrett's niece, Maude was hosting a top-rating radio show and fronting a television program about video games, and was once labelled 'Australia's sexiest geek' by *FHM* magazine. James and Maude knew each other after crossing paths at Foxtel and had undeniable chemistry. I had once recorded a mock segment with them at Seven to show senior executives, and chief executive Tim Worner agreed they had something special.

The show couldn't take itself too seriously. It would need to be fun and at times frivolous—like a good FM radio show. Such a model for breakfast television had worked before. *The Big Breakfast,* perhaps best known for Paula Yates's interviews conducted in bed, was a phenomenal ratings success for Britain's Channel 4 in the early 1990s. The show tapped into a younger mindset and knocked off its more serious competitors, *BBC Breakfast* and *GMTV.*

Ian Hogg thought the concept had merit but wondered whether Ten could afford it. The answer, I ventured, was an advertorial-based sister show. They were cash cows for Seven and Nine, and could subsidise any new tilt at breakfast by Ten. I had no real thoughts on what form it would take, apart from it needing to be different from my earlier creation at Seven, *The Morning Show.*

The idea of producing another breakfast show had been the last thing on my mind; Julian and I had only just been talking about heading to Hong Kong, Beijing or Shanghai. But the more Hogg's interest in my concept for Ten spiked, the more mine did as well. We talked about selling it to James Warburton as a Fremantle production. That would also ease some of the immediate cost burden on Ten.

James met with Hogg and me in the boardroom of Fremantle's St Leonards headquarters. By then, I was also ready to pitch a mid-morning show (featuring advertorials) based around the legendary Ita Buttrose. James liked both concepts but I suspect wouldn't have done the shows with a production company.

Ian Hogg was his usual gracious self and happy to wish me well; Paul Anstee and Julian urged me to consider other options. They'd heard me whinge about breakfast television and thought it was important for me to try something else. They were right but I went ahead anyway, for reasons to do with both loyalty and spite.

James Warburton had been one of my biggest supporters at Seven. Without him *The Morning Show* wouldn't have been on air. His problems at Ten were considerable; he was dealing with a legacy of bad management decisions that would take time to overcome. I wanted to do what I could to help. That desire was further fuelled by my rising bitterness towards Seven. I was upset I'd wasted the last few years on what I considered meaningless projects and that I'd been denied the chance to run a news division. Perhaps, I told myself, I wasn't over breakfast television at all, just Channel Seven. Those factors blinded me to something that should have been obvious: I'd be competing with shows I created and the team that I built. I now understand why people at *Sunrise* saw that as an act of betrayal.

Three days after shaking hands with James, I was walking through Sydney Airport when I looked up at a television. Sky News was reporting breaking news: James Warburton had been sacked by Channel Ten for failing to get instant results. I couldn't believe it. He'd been in the job for a little more than a year—nowhere near long enough to turn around a network. To this day, I consider the board's decision appalling.

The man taking over from James would be advertising hotshot Hamish McLennan. He'd run some of the biggest agencies in the world before working alongside Rupert Murdoch as a trusted adviser in New York. I met with Hamish two days before he flew back to America to pack up his home. It was obvious he couldn't wait to get to work. Eyes wide open and grinning from side to side of his face, he spoke as if he were letting me in on a grand plan. He told me we needed to fix things and that it was going to be one hell of a ride.

I walked him through the concept for the breakfast show, which I'd given the working title *Maude and Matho: Live from the Beach* and he instantly liked what he saw. Hamish had an infectious enthusiasm and the confidence of someone who'd made it big in New York. By the end of the meeting, he had me excited about returning to breakfast TV.

It seemed my little show on the beach was going to see life. And, in the process, it would almost cost me mine.

18

SURF AND TURF

Manda Hatter is a proud dyke on a bike—each year, she jumps aboard her Honda CBF 1000 to lead Sydney's Gay and Lesbian Mardi Gras. But that's not the only reason I love her. Manda was one of the first people I met at Channel Ten. As project manager for morning television, it was her job to turn my thought bubbles into reality.

We got to know each other on a casual drive to the beach. It was clear she was more comfortable on her bike than in her car, after she backed into the wall of a car park. She wasn't too fazed. Just like Dave Masala at Seven, she wasn't one to let setbacks slow her down. She maintained a very cool demeanour, while still managing to be tough when it counted.

We were on the hunt for *Maude and Matho'* s beachside home. We started at Coogee, in south-east Sydney, and worked our way north. We needed a building not just with a good view but that was big enough to house our studio. For the next few days, we went from pubs to penthouses to piers. Nothing much impressed us until we reached Manly and a surf club that was an institution. Located at the southern end of the beach, it had been there, in one form or another, since 1911. Many locals, including a woman in her sixties who cornered us on the day, had grown up with it. With skin like leather, she clearly wasn't kidding when she told us she spent most days at the beach. She was a character; the type who, as an unpaid extra, could make a real difference to our show.

We dropped in on another local character: Manly mayor Jean Hay. She'd lived in the suburb all her life and was first elected to council in 1987. There wasn't much about the area she didn't know. Councils can sometimes be a television show's worst enemy. Some are just too bureaucratic to bother with, while others squeeze you for every cent. Jean embraced us as old friends, though. Over tea and biscuits, she told us we were exactly what the area needed. We got the sense she also liked the idea of getting one up on Bondi Beach, which usually monopolised national attention.

Jean had a suggestion that would make a world of difference. The Manly Surf Club was about to close for renovations, but she pointed us to what she believed was a much better spot, at the other end of the beach. Queenscliff Surf Life Saving Club had already been made over and offered a stunning view of the ocean. She vowed to do whatever it took to have us move in there.

With *Maude and Matho* coming together, attention shifted to its sister show—the one that would bring in the cash. For obvious reasons, panel shows only work if you choose the right panellists.

Ita Buttrose would be the linchpin. Her record spoke for itself: she was the founding editor of *Cleo*, held the reins at *The Australian Women's Weekly* and was the first woman to head a metropolitan newspaper. She'd been immortalised in television dramas and a classic Aussie song. There really was no one like her.

My attempt to woo her got off to a disastrous start. She'd agreed to meet me for coffee at Sydney's Sheraton on the Park but a mix-up with my calendar meant I never showed up. After waiting fifteen minutes, she called to see where I was. I almost collapsed in embarrassment as I realised I'd just stood up Ita Buttrose. She was gracious enough to give me another chance.

I can only think of two people in my life I've genuinely felt nervous about meeting. Ita was one and the other was someone I'd grown up worshipping: Jana Wendt. I called Jana in 2006, hoping she'd be part of a special I was making to celebrate the birthday of Australian television. I must have sounded like a blithering idiot as I struggled to string together a sentence. She put me out of my misery by accepting. I'd vowed to do better when I sat down with Ita but, thankfully, she did most of the talking. She was warm, generous and, best of all, excited about my idea, revealing that hosting a television show was something she'd always wanted to do.

The rest of the panel consisted of Jessica Rowe, Sarah Harris, Joe Hildebrand and a daily mystery guest, to keep things fresh. The working title was *The Five* (but we'd later let viewers change the name to *Studio 10* via an online poll).

Sarah Harris was being wasted at Channel Nine, despite having a proven track record as both a reporter and presenter. The show's soon-to-be executive producer, Rob McKnight, argued strongly, and rightly, that she had a level of calm control that would enable her to steer the show from topic to topic as the panel mouthed off.

Joe Hildebrand had a knack for throwing grenades. A columnist with Sydney's *Daily Telegraph,* he often went out of his way to be controversial, but not in the way of a radio shock jock. He was simply cynical about life and didn't mind telling everyone why, but it was usually in the most hilarious of ways. Joe would be our cat among the pigeons.

Jessica Rowe is one of my favourite people, on and off television. During her time as newsreader on *Weekend Sunrise,* she'd been a passionate advocate for fairness and equality. Her trademark sense of optimism would help offset Joe.

With our shows taking shape and the presenting line-ups looking good, we would need to be backed by a strong team of producers. Pumping out five hours of content each day takes skill. Rob McKnight was one of the first people I called. Not only had I worked with him many times at Seven, I knew he was craving becoming an executive producer; his bosses at Nine had been resisting because he was seen as too valuable as a maker of promos for the network's news and current affairs programs. He seemed the perfect person to take control of *Studio 10.* 'It was a no-brainer for me,' says Rob. 'I always knew going to Ten would be a risk, but why should that ever stop anyone? People were saying, "Oh, you're crazy to leave such a cosy position at Nine," but I thought I'd be crazy not to give it a go.'

Two of my colleagues from *Weekend Sunrise* also made the switch, including entertainment producer Stefan Mitchell and Ciaran Flannery, who I wanted to be *Maude and Matho'* s supervising producer. A UK boy, Ciaran knew *The Big Breakfast* well. He told me that the opportunity of producing something similar in Australia was too good to pass up. Some original *Sunrise* staffers agreed to join my team, including Mark Dransfield, Fiona Fagan (who was based in London) and the supervising producer from our days in the old tin shed, Matt Clarke. It was like we were getting the band back together. There were plenty of fresh faces too. The younger ones reminded me of how I felt in the early days of *Sunrise*. They were clearly excited about building something from the ground up and working on a new type of show.

But the extent to which things would be new came into serious question in May 2013.

Hamish McLennan shifted Ten's entire focus. No longer was it a network chasing younger viewers but, rather, anyone who was 'young at heart'. In other words, Ten was about to target a very similar audience to the ones watching Seven and Nine. He had a solid argument. Ten's core audience of people aged between sixteen and forty-nine could no longer be counted on to deliver big ratings. Some had shifted their viewing habits to new digital stations like Go! and Eleven, while others were simply downloading their favourite shows. I just wished he'd come to that realisation before we'd set off on our course. Something like *The Big Breakfast* would no longer suit; James Mathison and Maude Garrett were not just young at heart but young in every other respect. The show would need to be completely rethought.

And here's where I went wrong.

Instead of starting from scratch, I held on to key features from the original plan, including both the beach studio and James. I was so against the idea of producing another *Sunrise* that I tried to force a square peg into a round hole. Peter Meakin, who'd soon follow me to Ten, to become the network's new head of news and current affairs, believes it was a serious mistake. 'You were too adventurous,' he tells me. 'I can see the temptation of not cloning or going head to head with the two dinosaurs, but that's what you really had to do.' Instead, we became a halfway house. Maude would become our Hollywood correspondent, while James would get a new co-host:

someone who had a more serious image, who could cover big news stories.

While we considered who that might be, most of our attention was on hosts at a different network. In early July, Melissa Doyle announced she was leaving *Sunrise* after a remarkable fourteen years. I couldn't help but wonder whether it was really her choice. Those in the know at Seven (including those *not* paid to turn fiction into fact) tell me it absolutely was. She realised what we knew to be true: nobody can stay on one show forever. Her new role as a primetime anchor was bound to give her new life. It also gave Michael Pell the chance to do what he'd been waiting to do: appoint Samantha Armytage as the show's new co-host. Kochie and Mel became Kochie and Sam.

Kochie and Mel weren't the only ones breaking up (at least, on air—they remain close and have dinner on the same Thursday of every month)—Julian and I also decided to part ways. I couldn't ask him to wait for me any longer and, after years of false starts, Julian finally moved to Hong Kong (where he's now working for one of the city's top design firms). He was off to take on the world, while I was back doing morning TV. Still, Julian will always be one of my closest friends.

With work on the beachside studio underway, we began auditioning co-hosts for James. We had no set view on who that should be; our thinking had been shifted so dramatically that we had very open minds.

Although we tried people from all over Australia, there were two women from Ten's own newsroom in Sydney we kept coming back to. As one of the network's most prominent newsreaders, Natarsha Belling was the best known of the pair. Smooth, warm and with almost flawless presenting skills, Tarsh had worked hard to gain her reputation. Natasha Exelby, though also a newsreader, was more unpredictable. In early 2013, she made headlines after flirting with a guest on air and then laughing about it during a story about riots in Brazil. Her sense of mischief was what I liked. She and Natarsha may have worked in the same newsroom, but that was about all they had in common. And both gelled well with James but in very different ways. Tarsh brought out his conservative side (they bonded easily over parenting) while Natasha tapped his more edgy persona (they had a robust discussion about sex). Given Ten's new direction, the most logical choice for co-host was Tarsh, but there was something about Natasha that we couldn't quite shake. She had a rawness about her that I found especially appealing. She shot from the hip and said what she felt, no matter what others might think.

Before making a call, we tried one last thing. What would it look like if we kept *both* Tarsh and Natasha alongside James? As it turned out, it was a question worth asking. The three-host dynamic really did work. We recorded weeks of tests that left few in doubt about their chemistry. Natasha and Tarsh would easily pick up discussions where the other left off, while

James delivered reasoned arguments with compassion. One exchange in particular stood out: a ten-minute debate about politics. Tarsh and Natasha argued about whether Tony Abbott was sexist while James dissected each of his then policies. It was smart, funny and different; everyone who saw it agreed it was what commercial television needed. Ciaran and I felt that if they could repeat that dynamic on air, our show's new direction wouldn't be so bad. James Mathison, Natarsha Belling and Natasha Exelby were soon announced as the hosts of Ten's new breakfast show, now called *Wake Up.* (We almost called it *Wake Up Call* but James argued against it.)

But we weren't done yet. From my experience at *Sunrise,* I knew that Melbourne would need special attention. I worried about how locals would perceive a breakfast show from what was obviously a Sydney beach. The answer, I thought, was to set up a second studio in Melbourne's Federation Square. Nuala Hafner would use it each day to read the show's half-hourly news. I'd known Nuala for years. She'd performed all types of roles at *Sunrise,* from London correspondent to weather presenter to entertainment editor. Her versatility wasn't limited to on air, either. She'd started her career as a lawyer, and when I approached her about joining *Wake Up,* she was almost done with a psychology degree. I wanted everyone on the show to have intelligence, humour and compassion. Nuala had all three in spades.

The final product may not have resembled our original strategy but we were determined to give it everything we had. And, besides, we'd still look different from Seven and Nine. We even had a beach!

I pointed out those differences to anyone who asked. In an interview with media website *mUmBRELLA*, I insisted that *Sunrise* and *Today* had become so similar to each other that viewers struggled to tell them apart. And I went further, condemning both shows for what I considered their newfound fear of taking risks. Those remarks hurt many of the people I'd spent more than a decade working alongside. David Koch later told me he thought my comments lacked class. He was right. Taking such swipes is something I deeply regret.

Interviews like that certainly created a noise, though. One of the reasons those of us involved with the show kept doing them was because of our concern that otherwise we'd be drowned out. The show's marketing consisted mainly of a sporadic run of commercials on our own station; given Ten's primetime ratings were lagging well behind Seven's, Nine's and, usually, the ABC's, that wasn't going to be a significant help.

We also launched an aggressive grassroots campaign on social media, with the rallying call 'I'm Ready for Change'. I wanted *Wake Up* to engage with our audience around the clock, instead of just when the show was on air. Twitter hooked me up with its head of media integration in New York, Fred Graver, who'd worked on everything from the Travel Channel to *Late Night with David Letterman.* He helped build a strategy that would need a small team to execute, so we hired three producers with the sole task of handling social media—all under thirty and all just as happy in the online world as in the real one. A member of that group was perhaps the most prolific tweeter I'd ever encountered. Kenny Ang posted about everything from Cher to the uprising in Egypt. It would be an unusual week if one of his tweets didn't pop up on screen during the ABC's *Q&A.*

He was smart and caring but had a sometimes-searing wit. And, unlike me, he was remarkably disciplined. There was much to like about Kenny but he made it clear to all who asked that he wasn't looking for love. The same couldn't be said about me. In the end, I think, I wore Kenny down. We began dating in October and discovered that as different as we were, we had just as many things in common, not least sharing the same mental illness. He, too, had bipolar.

In the weeks leading up to the show's launch, Kenny and I worked the overnight shift, turning up each day at 2am. It was the first time I'd worked such hours since my twenties. Our lack of resources wasn't helping matters; I was running the department, serving as *Wake Up'*s executive producer, and would be writing much of the show and putting it to air. It was pointless complaining, given it was my fault we'd set things up that way.

When *Wake Up* made its debut on Monday, 4 November, a friend called to ask whether I was okay. She'd seen a photo of me in the *Australian* that she thought made me look 'half-dead'. Things weren't that bad but I was certainly tired. The photo accompanied a story by Darren Davidson. He'd asked about early expectations for the show, to which I responded, 'We will have to get through some hard times.'

When I said it, I had no way of knowing just how true that would be.

19

WAKE UP CALL

'Standby, everyone. Five, four, three, two...'

The floor manager counted down to what we hoped would be a new era in breakfast television. It was a perfect Manly morning; surfers were catching a break while the sun rose on the horizon behind them. Our opening shot captured the feel perfectly. The camera swept from across the headland to reveal Tarsh, James and Natasha standing on the balcony of the Queenscliff Surf Life Saving Club. 'Good morning, everyone,' said a beaming Tarsh, 'and welcome to beautiful Manly Beach, and can you believe this is our new home?'

Signs of the show's split personality appeared in the first few minutes. As the hosts prepared to talk about the news of the day, a crew member walked in front of them carrying a surfboard. I'd approved it but it would have left some people wondering whether they were watching a news-based program or an FM radio show. That was a question we hadn't resolved ourselves.

And the program had a bigger problem: the much-hyped chemistry between the hosts was missing. They were understandably nervous but, at times, looked unsure who should be speaking, or, worse, were not talking at all. That left some on the team, including me, particularly worried. I agreed with media writers, such as the *Guardian'*s Amanda Meade, who labelled the first show 'clunky'. It wasn't just because of the presenters; the rundown itself seemed to lack flow. I left the control room feeling agitated and despondent.

It shouldn't have upset me as much as it did—the first day on air is never easy and live talk-based shows need a few weeks to iron out their wrinkles. And, as important as first impressions are, we weren't expecting many people to actually watch us on our debut. As then *Today* show boss Neil Breen said of us to an audience of students at the Australian Film, Television and Radio School, 'The biggest problem they have is that they're on Channel Ten.'

Hamish McLennan was happy with the first outings of both *Wake Up* and *Studio 10*; the latter certainly had a better feel (which was a real credit to its executive producer, Rob McKnight). Lachlan Murdoch was pleased too. He left a message on my phone, saying the team should all be proud. I didn't take his call because I was struggling to control my thoughts. Rather than sharing everyone's first-day enthusiasm, I became withdrawn. Kenny, who was already worried about my state of mind before the show started, urged me to get some rest.

That proved difficult. My mind seemed trapped, similar to how I felt when we launched *The Morning Show* back in 2007. I have no memory of what I was thinking later that night but I know I got no sleep. By the time I arrived for work at 2am the next day I resembled, as Kenny said, a zombie. He told me to get through the show and he'd take me home straight afterwards. He kept a close eye on me all morning and tried to shield me from people. There is nothing more useless than an executive producer who fails to lead his team, especially after just one day on air.

That morning's show remains little more than a blur. I sat in the control room without any control at all. People looked at me for instructions but I gave them little in return. Kenny sat next to me throughout and kept a firm but discreet hand on my leg. Towards the end of the show, he whispered, 'Half an hour more and then I'll get you out of here.' First-day ratings came out shortly after the show aired but I didn't hang around long enough to find out how many people had tuned in for our debut. Kenny told me to keep my head down and head straight to the car. He ran up to my office, grabbed my belongings and took me straight back to his apartment in Kings Cross. It turned out around 52000 people had watched our opening show, not far off our day-one forecast of 60000. McLennan told media writers, 'It's a two-year deal for us, so in no way did we think we were going to do anything more than the numbers we got.'

I was now completely cut off from my team. Kenny tried to sit me down for lunch but I was in and out of the conversation, restlessly wandering around his apartment, mumbling, 'Get me out, get me out.' Producers were calling every fifteen minutes but I wanted to hide.

Seclusion was not an option later that night.

We ended up at my unit in The Rocks and Kenny tried to calm me. I was rambling and pacing without even seeing him. I'd move from the bed to the floor and then back again. Nowhere felt safe. I apparently kept yelling, 'I'm trapped! I'm trapped!' before pacing some more. Lights seemed brighter than normal and I was startled by even the slightest of sounds. For a while I crawled around on the floor with a quilt covering my head and other times I backed into walls in a panic. I cried, screamed and often struggled to breathe.

After a few hours, Kenny fell asleep, convinced I'd started to settle down. But before long, I was again up and walking but this time in a more dire direction. We were thirteen levels above the street and I knew our balcony offered an escape—from my thoughts *and* my life. I stepped towards it with more focus than I'd shown in two days. As I neared it, I pulled myself back before again moving forward. At some point, something flickered at the back of my mind, like a light trying to break through the darkness. It offered just enough time for me to wake Kenny. In one of my few moments of clarity that night, I told him I needed to go to a hospital, and he could tell by my face he needed to call an ambulance quickly.

Police arrived before the paramedics and the three of them tried their best to keep me talking. It was Melbourne Cup day, so they asked if I'd had anything to drink or whether I'd been able to place a bet. I struggled to understand what they were saying and preferred to stay on the ground with my face in my hands. When the first paramedic walked through the door, she blurted out, 'Oh, I know you, Adam, I've dealt with you before! You're that guy from *Sunrise!*' I screamed and recoiled towards the wall as police moved in to restrain me. I'd spent two days trying to hide, not be recognised.

I was taken to Sydney's St Vincent's Hospital, where a nurse placed me in a small room with the lights switched off, so as to ease the strain on my eyes. Kenny and I sat and waited in that room for two hours, as nurses came in and out to take blood or offer me a cup of water. I was given drugs and knocked out. I slept for fourteen hours, with Kenny by my bedside the entire time. By the time I woke up the next afternoon, the resident psychologists assessed me and I was placed in the hospital's Psychiatric Emergency Care Centre—a place I never want to see again. With white walls and without windows, the only thing I could hear was the sound of a ticking clock. It did nothing to relieve the feeling of being trapped.

After I got released from the hospital (which, given mental health laws, was no easy task), we eventually managed to see the man who had first diagnosed me with bipolar, in 2007. Professor Gordon Parker put me back on medication I should've been taking for years. He said my mind needed time to reset and warned against rushing back to work. My mother was in constant contact with Kenny throughout the ordeal and suggested I spend time recovering at her home in Havannah Harbour, which is about forty minutes' drive from Vanuatu's capital, Port Vila. Rob McKnight couldn't have agreed more that I needed to rest and told me not to worry about the shows. He urged me to go Vanuatu and get well, and stepped in immediately as executive producer of *Wake Up* while continuing to run *Studio 10.* I know doing double duty took a toll on him and I was, and will always be, grateful for his protection and support.

What had been happening to me was terrific fodder for gossip writers. Some, like the *Daily Telegraph'* s Annette Sharp, treated it sensitively. She once told me that, at heart, she wasn't an arsehole, she'd just found herself in an arsehole's job. Others, like the *Sydney Morning Herald'* s Andrew Hornery, considered my mental illness an excuse and even said I'd made 'a public spectacle of a condition'. He implied that I was off on a tropical holiday so that I could desert a sinking ship. While articles like his can, of course, be hurtful, I think most people see them for what they are. As Hornery himself once wrote: 'A common complaint I have long heard is, "Why don't you write nice things?" to which I respond: "I write what people want to read." Your question just proves that no one remembers the nice stories, just the scandalous ones.' He's perhaps right but I do think journalists need to be careful about the impact their words can have on people who are already close to the edge. At the time, I was lucky to have Kenny hide from me everything that had been written.

But, even without seeing the articles, I knew I couldn't stay in Vanuatu. Despite people at Ten, including Hamish McLennan, urging me to take as much time as I needed, I felt an obligation to get back to my team. Kenny told me I was in no condition to return, given that I struggled to even watch the show. But others at the network *had* been watching closely and I felt had growing concerns over Natasha Exelby.

She'd become the odd one out on air. Tarsh and James would often be in full conversational flow when Natasha would interject with something that brought everything to a screeching halt. James turned to her on air one morning and said, 'I have absolutely no idea what you're talking about.' He did it in such a way as to solicit a laugh, but it pointed to an underlying problem: James and Tarsh felt a serious disconnect from Natasha. In truth, that was as much their fault as hers. I suspect they'd become so nervous about what she might say that they preferred her to say as little as possible.

Once chemistry is broken, it becomes very hard to repair. I felt we'd reached the point of no return and the only solution was to drop Natasha from the show.

I drove to Manly to see her on my first day back at work. It's never easy to deliver bad news, especially to someone you like. Natasha was, and remains, terrific talent and an even better person. The blame for her stilted performance lay more with me than her or her co-hosts. Had I been guiding the show through its early stages on air, I may have been able to stop the presenter dynamic from being derailed.

I met with Natasha straight after the show, in my car as we overlooked the beach. I didn't want her to go to Channel Ten, where I thought the cold formality of a meeting with HR would undermine what I wanted to be a personal explanation. I suspect she knew it was coming. Although visibly and understandably upset, Natasha agreed the show hadn't been working. Her last wish was that I'd stop it from becoming just another breakfast show. 'Be different,' she told me, 'just like you'd promised.'

The problem, though, was that by removing Natasha, we'd removed another point of difference. The uniqueness of a three-presenter model was replaced by a traditional male and female combination. Still, as sorry as they felt for Natasha, I had the feeling that James and Tarsh were relieved, hoping my decision would allow them to be themselves.

I tried my best to get back to business, but found myself avoiding even simple duties, like daily production meetings. I struggled to be around people and felt the black dog back by my side. Less than a week after returning to work, my mind again surrendered to my illness. I was sitting in Rob McKnight's office when he noticed my speech slow, eyes well up and body begin to shake. He told Kenny to take me home.

I was placed back in the care of Gordon Parker but I don't even remember seeing him. He later said it was like I wasn't in the room. I'd lost weight and colour, and his diagnosis was that I had biological melancholic depression. After being placed on an even stronger cocktail of drugs, I wanted nothing more than to stay in bed. I slept from 5pm to 4pm the following day. For the sake of my wellbeing and that of the show, I felt I had no choice but to resign. That was the most difficult thing of all. I knew I'd let down my team; they needed a leader but I was now anything but. I also let down the network. McLennan, in particular, had been good to me from the day we met to the day I left.

I decided, too, that I wasn't just walking away from Ten but from commercial television altogether. I announced my decision with a self-indulgent post on Facebook (which I knew would be picked up media writers). I waxed lyrical about my achievements in television and how I felt I had nothing else to prove. On reflection, I consider the post a slap in the face to people who'd followed me to Ten and to the network itself. I was essentially saying I couldn't care less about them and that everything I needed to do was done. I think I was just too embarrassed to acknowledge the truth: I was no longer strong enough to compete and felt humiliated by my weakness.

Kenny and I had no real plan apart from trying to fix me. I enrolled to study international relations at university and started learning Pilates. I liked the idea of working on both my mind and my body. Not long after, the ABC's *Australian Story* approached me about documenting my breakdown. I said no at first, preferring to step away from the public eye. But the more they spoke to me, the more I came to accept that it could help counter the stigma around mental illness—the stigma that results in half of all Australians conceding they'd prefer to avoid people who have such illnesses. That attitude does nothing to ease an even worse statistic: forty-four people take their lives every week in this country and someone attempts to do so every ten minutes. It's clear we have a major problem and one that doesn't get talked about enough.

I was in the United States the day *Australian Story* was set to air. On that same day, the *Australian* newspaper printed an email I'd sent to David Leckie, Peter Meakin and Michael Pell back in 2011. It revealed what it called my secret plan to axe David Koch (and others) from *Sunrise.* The timing was no accident: it was meant to cause harm while some were feeling empathy for my plight. And it worked. It triggered a severe anxiety attack and I collapsed on the floor of my hotel room in Washington. I felt sick that people I'd already hurt at *Sunrise* would now consider this the final straw.

Miraculously, emails sent by other executives at the time weren't leaked along with mine. The fact the senders still worked at Seven probably had something to do with that. (I have no reason to believe Leckie, Meakin or Michael leaked my email, and I know it was sent to other news executives.) It says much about the nature of commercial television that the person behind the leak was so determined to damage me that he didn't care the *Sunrise* presenting team would suffer too. I reached out to some of those named in my email, in the hope of making them understand the context in which it was sent.

The next morning, *Sunrise* 'set the record straight' on air. Kochie told viewers (who I'm sure couldn't have cared less about the story) that the email had been written by 'some bloke called Adam Boland who wasn't even working on the show'. Samantha Armytage then chimed in, calling the story 'a big steaming pile of poo'. Kochie agreed, before adding, 'Saner heads prevailed.' Natalie backed it up with 'Much more sane minds stepped in', before Armytage rounded things off with 'Of course they were more sane'. Mark Beretta remained quiet throughout.

Given their rant came just ten hours after *Australian Story* had detailed my battle with mental illness, their choice of words was always going to garner attention. Kate Leaver led the backlash, with a scathing piece on *Mamamia*: 'To imply that Adam Boland's sanity was not intact when he worked at Channel Seven—the morning after his deeply personal *Australian Story* aired—is inexcusable. The wink-wink-nudge-nudge emphasis each of the hosts placed on the words "sane" and "sanity" was no accident.'

I like to think it was an accident, particularly as far as Kochie and Nat are concerned. If anything, I was more upset by Kochie's use of the phrase 'some bloke called Adam Boland'. As one original *Sunrise* producer said to me, 'I don't know who those people are any more.' Perhaps they didn't know who *I* was any more.

***

Despite publicly giving *Wake Up* a two-year commitment, Channel Ten swung the axe. The show went to air for the final time on Friday, 23 May. Tarsh struggled to get though the final minutes. As she broke down, James declared, in the way that only he could, 'Let's hug it out, bitches!'

Viewers were dismayed by Ten's decision, and their comments flooded the network's Facebook page. One wrote: 'You want everything in a hurry. 6 months is all you gave this show. You never gave them a chance. For god's sake, Rome wasn't built in a day. Glad you don't run the business I work in.' Many had developed affection for both James and Tarsh. Another posted: 'James, I applaud you for being such an articulate, compassionate and humorous man. Natarsha, such a great role model of an intelligent, modern woman. Hope to see you all back on TV soon.

Commentators who'd stuck with the show agreed. Tim Burrowes wrote on *mUmBRELLA* that 'the failure of the show is not about content. It's in large part about the inability of the network to successfully persuade people to watch it.'

That was part of the problem, but something else was at play.

Media analyst Steve Allen says Seven and Nine were just too strong: 'Sunrise and Today defended their ground supremely. They threw a lot of money in cross promotion to ensure they didn't leak audience and they gave away substantial amounts of cash prizes, the likes of which we'd rarely seen in that timeslot.' The *Sunrise* cash cow went from being a monthly novelty to a daily member of the team. And the show's primetime promotion was unprecedented. Kochie and Sam kept popping up in top-rating shows like *My Kitchen Rules,* the kind of exposure *Sunrise* would have killed for just a few years earlier. (These were facts ignored by some press coverage that implied Melissa Doyle's departure from *Sunrise* was the sole reason for the show's ratings having become more stable.)

Nine and Seven weren't just trying to get rid of *Wake Up,* they were also going hammer and tongs at each other. The slot remained one of the most competitive on television, and this was all the more reason *Wake Up* should've been aimed at a younger audience. But, despite everything it had going against it, *Wake Up* showed signs of green shoots in its final months. It had become a very different show from the one I'd clumsily launched, and the team had worked even harder to overcome early setbacks and no resources. They delivered a show with heart. Research conducted by one of Ten's rivals just weeks before its axing revealed that positive perceptions of *Wake Up* had dramatically increased. Television history proves that perceptions always change before behaviour does.

But even if *Wake Up* didn't reach its audience targets, Ten had maintained to everyone it was committed to breakfast television. There wasn't the slightest sign of the production team being shown the door.

So, what caused such a radical change of heart? What caused Hamish McLennan to breach his two-year commitment without any warning?

The answer can be found in something else Ten decided at the same time. *Wake Up* wouldn't be the only show to go. Ten also cancelled morning and late night news bulletins. In all, 150 people lost their jobs, including some long-serving middle managers. It was a savage cut that extended well beyond breakfast. Not even news boss Peter Meakin saw it coming. He said to me it was one of the worst days of his life and told the media he was now an admiral without a fleet.

It seemed as if something had caused Ten to panic. Steve Allen says there was no doubt: 'We've said if they don't have a 22 per cent share of the overall audience, they can't make money. And that's what was happening.'

Channel Ten paid $100 million for rights to cricket's Big Bash League. A lot of money, but it was a move that made sense. Channel Seven had long used its high-rating coverage of the Australian Open to launch new seasons of programming. The theory being that viewers will stick around for shows they've seen constantly advertised during the tennis.

Ten's hopes were not just pinned on the cricket but on its almost simultaneous coverage of the Sochi Olympics. It was a big summer of sport for Ten, which should have served as the perfect springboard for new primetime shows. But it didn't. Big hope *So You Think You Can Dance* was attracting just 330000 viewers on a Sunday night, compared with 1.2 million viewers for *60 Minutes* and the 1.5 million people watching Seven's *My Kitchen Rules*. Even shows that had received critical acclaim, like the dramas *Puberty Blues* and *Secrets & Lies* failed to meet their ratings expectations.

Hamish McLennan's disappointment was clear when he spoke to *Business Spectator'*s Alan Kohler: 'Look, I would've hoped for more of a halo effect.' With no sign of a turnaround, Steve Allen says they were left with no choice. 'They couldn't make money. They looked at their ratings and how the sales force can monetise those ratings and they've gone, "Right, we just can't make money with our current overheads."'

Those overheads didn't just include staff and the cost of making programs but high licence fees paid to the federal government. McLennan thinks it's becoming increasingly difficult for Australian networks to compete with online media. As he told Alan Kohler: 'They minimise their tax. They domicile themselves in offshore havens and we pay our corporate tax, we pay licence fees, we've got commitments to local productions ... so the sum total of all of that is that we're under pressure.'

For Ten to be profitable, not only does it need to be on a level playing field, it needs a better armoury of programming. Channel Seven turned its fortunes around in 2005 off the back of American imports *Desperate Housewives* and *Grey's Anatomy*. Those shows were tent poles for its entire programming line-up. As Michael Lallo wrote in *The Age*: 'The absence of a tent pole show ... can precipitate a downward spiral that's hard to correct.' Ten didn't have even one tent pole, let alone two.

While I was relieved that *Studio 10* was spared, I was bitterly disappointed on behalf of the staff at *Wake Up*. And, despite Ten's broader problems, I couldn't help but think the show might have stood a better chance if I'd been able to do my job. Some of the key producers left secure positions after assurances from me that Ten was committed to at least two years of breakfast television.

Two of those people were Fiona Fagan and Mark Dransfield. Both had played significant roles in the success of Seven's morning programming: Mark was a former supervising producer of *Sunrise,* while Fiona had overseen the launch of *The Morning Show.* They never got caught up in network politics and found joy from just making good telly. Their departure from Seven wasn't a result of lack of loyalty to the network but of loyalty to me.

After their sacking from Ten, and without their knowledge, I reached out to Michael Pell, with a text that read simply: 'There are some very good people out of work—not the least being Fiona and Drano (Mark). They came to Ten because I asked them. Don't hold that against them. If you have freelance work (or whatever), please remember they're not only excellent producers, they're also very good people.'

I was disappointed to see that text not only leaked to the *Australian* newspaper but reported in such a one-sided way. Media gossip writer Sharri Markson wrote that Michael 'was less than impressed about being told what to do by Boland, who had badmouthed him around town, and continues to take full credit for *Sunrise'*s success—a sentiment that frustrates almost every senior executive at the Seven Network'.

The fact I have left so many people in television hating me (including some, like Michael, who once loved me) has, naturally, forced me to reflect. I'm proud of many things I did during my time in television and, in particular, the activism of *Sunrise* and its original charter to make a difference. I'm not proud of the way I made that happen: an almost single-minded devotion to my shows that sometimes blinded me to the way I treated those around me.

Throughout my life, television was the constant—be it hounding reporters when I was a child or creating shows when I was an adult. It took me far too long to realise there's so much more to life, and that life is indeed worth living. As Peter Meakin put it on *Australian Story,* 'I think a lot of people in television are partially deranged.'

Time will tell if leaving television helps me put myself back together again.

BACK COVER MATERIAL

'I thought I knew a bit about breakfast TV. I was wrong. What we see is nothing compared to what goes on behind the scenes. I was fascinated to read this brutally honest account of so many stories that have become Australian media folklore. The characters, the drama, the egos. It is an unflinching account from the man who has arguably had a greater impact on the way we watch TV than anyone since Graham Kennedy.'
MIA FREEDMAN

Between *Sunrise* and *The Morning Show*, Adam Boland oversaw thirty hours of network television a week, turning a daggy finance nerd and a suburban mum into household names. He even helped propel Kevin Rudd into The Lodge.

Now, for the first time, he takes us behind the camera, inside the *Sunrise* family. *Brekky Central* is the story of the most competitive timeslot on television; the stakes are high and so are the pressures on those who show up each morning to win the ratings. Along the way, celebrities do what celebrities do, television executives outmanoeuvre each other and presenters succeed or fail.

This is a world of hellishly long hours, of silliness and seriousness, an extraordinary mix of egos, scandals and drama but also a celebration of the magic that is television.

Printed in Great Britain
by Amazon